MBA Admission
FOR SMARTIES

The No-Nonsense Guide to
Acceptance at Top Business Schools

MBA Admission
FOR SMARTIES

The No-Nonsense Guide to
Acceptance at Top Business Schools

By Linda Abraham and Judy Gruen

Accepted.com
Los Angeles, California

ACCEPTED

www.accepted.com

Accepted.com
Los Angeles, California
www.accepted.com
310-815-9553

ISBN 1466294981

Library of Congress Control number 2011916022

First Edition

Printed in the United States

10 9 8 7 6 5 4 3 2 1

To my parents and my husband, who have
inspired, encouraged, and sustained.

– Linda Abraham

To Jeff, my husband and best friend, my love forever.

– Judy Gruen

CONTENTS

Preface 1

PART 1
SETTING YOUR STRATEGY

1 Objective MBA: Let Your Goals Guide You 7

2 How to Research MBA Programs and
Why It's Essential That You Do...17

3 How Qualified Are You?..33

4 Choosing the Right Schools for *You* 49

PART 2
PRESENTING YOURSELF AS A WINNING CANDIDATE

5 Writing for Acceptance...61

6 How to Handle Specific Essay Types: Goals, Achievement/
Leadership, Failure, Personal Influences and Optional Essays....85

7 13 Rules for Resumes that Rock..111

8 How to Gather Fabulous Letters of Recommendation.........125

9 Prepare to Shine During Interviews 141

10 Tips for Special Applicants: Waitlisted, Reapplicants, Career
Changers, Military, Overrepresented Groups, Underrepresented
Minorities, Older Applicants, Younger Applicants.................155

Afterword: After You Hit "Send" 177

Preface

If you are considering adding the prestigious initials "MBA" to your credentials, you are probably like many of the thousands of clients my graduate school admissions company, Accepted.com, has worked with over the years: intelligent, goal-oriented, ambitious and eager to make your mark in the world of business. Whether you dream of bringing new products to the marketplace, becoming a successful investment banker or one day having the title of CEO of a business or not-for-profit organization, you know that a robust business education can make the difference between realizing those dreams – or not.

It's no wonder that in good economic times or bad, the MBA remains one of the most sought-after graduate degrees. Foundational coursework in business combined with access to internships, specialty programs and powerful alumni networks usually makes the investment in an MBA pay off handsomely. Research commissioned by *Bloomberg Businessweek* in 2011 and conducted by PayScale estimated the difference in median cash compensation (salary and bonuses) between the "haves" and "have-nots" of MBAs to be more than $1 million over the course of twenty years. And you won't be surprised to learn that the most prestigious of the full-time MBA programs, including Harvard, Wharton and Stanford, yielded a long-term salary differential much greater, about $3.6 million over a twenty-year period. That's a lot of cash.

But here's what you may not know: Gaining acceptance to the right MBA programs for you requires considerable thought, research and effort – significantly more than you may realize. Notice that I said *the right MBA programs for you* and not the most illustrious name in the pantheon of top-ranked programs. MBA applicants like to aim as high as possible when applying to schools, but even in tougher economic times it's always a buyer's market, and the MBA programs are the buyers. This is one reason, though certainly not the only reason, why *the process of choosing an MBA program must go beyond a superficial picking of the top ten or even top twenty schools.*

In more than sixteen years as a graduate school admissions consultant, I have seen a needless yet predictable pattern in too many clients. These men and women were well qualified for many excellent programs yet set themselves up for rejection by failing to evaluate how closely they fit with their target schools, which were often out of their league. Dazzled by a school's star status, these applicants didn't or wouldn't explore whether they were competitive for their "reach" schools or even whether the schools met their educational needs. I am not suggesting that you shouldn't aim high, but you're much more likely to hit your target if you subscribe to the "Ready, Aim, Fire!" approach rather than the "Fire, Aim!" approach.

Fortunately, most of our clients understand that to be successful in their quest for an MBA, they must ask themselves two fundamental questions:

☑ Do my career goals and personal preferences match the school's curricular, extracurricular, and recruiting strengths?

☑ Do my academic and professional qualifications compare favorably to the school's recent class profiles?

When you take the time and effort to match your career goals to the school strengths, you reveal "fit," an element all admissions committee members look for. When you understand how your profile compares to those recently accepted, you are in a position to evaluate your competitiveness for a particular program. The schools that help you achieve your goals are the ones you should want to attend, and the schools where you are competitive are those more likely to accept you. Determining overlap between those two categories will help open the MBA admissions doors at the right schools for you.

An effective application is not about spin

It's also become popular among some grad school consultants to claim that MBA candidates need to create "spin" in their applications and advise candidates to "brand" themselves. I disagree. Branding is important for consumer products, like Pepsi, Patagonia, and Puma, and it's essential for ranchers who need to identify their cattle. Spin is also necessary after publicity disasters or to put the best face on poor corporate earnings. Ultimately, however, no matter how competitive a program is, the MBA applications process involves complex and multifaceted human beings on the admissions committee who are carefully (albeit sometimes quickly) evaluating other complex and multi-faceted human beings as potential matches for their programs.

Understood this way, focusing on spin is a bad idea not only because it is simplistic and artificial. It's a bad idea because in focusing on the sizzle rather than the steak, you might easily present yourself in a way that is inauthentic or incomplete. Either scenario is a loser for you. For example, let's say you portray yourself as someone you *think* the school wants you to be (but are not) and are accepted. In that case, you may realize only too late that the school is a bad fit for the real you. This emphasis on marketing over authentic presentation will likely cause you to miss opportunities to reveal yourself to the admissions committee in a meaningful way. This, sadly, can dash your prospects for acceptance. So leave the spin for the wash cycle and branding for soft drinks and athletic shoes. Your job as an MBA applicant is to show yourself to full advantage – authentically and genuinely.

What this book will help you accomplish

When the admissions committee sees that you aren't a fit, you're toast. So it's not enough to aim high; you have to aim *smart*. That's why I'm glad you have picked up this book. *MBA Admissions for Smarties* will be your friendly guide to *both* aspects of a successful application: the *strategy* involved in research-ing appropriate schools and the effective *presentation* of your candidacy. The greatest boost to your odds for acceptance requires *beginning with the end goal in mind*. In Part 1 of this book, I will show you how to map out a winning strategy that will help you:

- ☑ Define and assess your career goals.

- ☑ Determine which MBA programs should remain on your target list.

- ☑ Assess your qualifications, both quantitatively and qualitatively.

- ☑ Evaluate fit with the program, which leapfrogs you ahead of much of the competition.

- ☑ Decide how many schools to apply to and when to apply.

In Part 2, we will move from the strategy to presentation. In these chapters I will show you how to present your qualifications clearly, compellingly and authentically. Specifically, you will learn how to:

- ☑ Develop core ideas for your essays and build each one with meaningful, distinctive content.

- ☑ Avoid the most common pitfalls of weak or forgettable essays.

- ☑ Respond to particular essay questions.

- ☑ Edit for quality, cohesiveness and authenticity.

- ☑ Write and revise your resume for maximum impact and minimum fat.

- ☑ Gather letters of recommendation that pack a punch.

- ☑ Prepare for school interviews.

Tailor your applications for special circumstances (i.e., waitlisted, reapplicant, overrepresented applicant pool, underrepresented minority, career changers, military, older or younger applicants).

At Accepted.com, we work with our clients to help them think through their strategy and make their strongest case for admission. In *MBA Admissions for Smarties*, I am sharing the winning strategies that have proven themselves over time and helped earn admission for thousands of clients to top programs in the United States and internationally. This book offers practical advice on how to present yourself to the schools to maximum advantage, with minimal headaches and second-guessing.

A few notes on the text: While this book was written by both of us, we have chosen to write it using the singular "I" instead of "we" for a friendlier, personal feel. Additionally, all names of clients have been changed.

Behind the scenes, you not only benefit from two experienced admissions consultants, but also from several other Accepted.com editors whose contributions have added so much to this book. Jennifer Bloom, Natalie Grinblatt Epstein, Cindy Tokumitsu, and former Accepted.com editor Dr. Sachin

Waikar all allowed us to excerpt their blog posts and offered their expertise. Nancy Evans went far beyond the call of duty in bringing her many years of experience in textbook development editing to this project. Her recommendations on both style and content have added tremendous value, and Dr. Rebecca Blustein offered expert proofreading in the final stages.

Aside from our own talented staff, Maxx Duffy, founder of Maxx Associates; Dr. Christie St. John, Senior Associate Director of Admission at the Tuck School of Business; Leila Pirnia, Founder of MBA Podcaster; and Christine Sneva, Director, Admissions and Financial Aid at the Johnson Graduate School of Management read the manuscript in draft form and offered valuable feedback.

And now, let's get started!

Linda Abraham and Judy Gruen

Chapter 1

Objective MBA:
Let Your Goals Guide You

"If you don't know where you are going, you might wind up someplace else." -- **Yogi Berra**

I had spent the day at a leading strategy consulting firm giving a seminar on MBA admissions. My presentation was well-received, and I had a good time. I was simultaneously exhausted and energized.

Thinking back on the day, I realized that in each of the four presentations I delivered, whether talking about applicant qualifications, choosing schools, the admissions perspective, or planning for the future, I ended up talking about the importance of goals. And in the afternoon when meeting individually with future applicants, I was struck by the fact that *none* of them had clear goals for their MBA, not even the ones who were definitely committed to applying in the coming fall and were working hard on GMAT prep.

Here's a perfect example. A young man named Alex[1] approached me, keen to discuss his MBA application strategy and target schools. Alex was also eager to tell me about his GMAT (720), his work experience as an engineer at a start-up and, more recently, his experience at an established software company, where he devised a creative solution that saved the firm nearly $75,000 in streamlined efficiencies during the last year. Alex had a respectable community service track record as a Big Brother and tutor. He was a strong candidate on paper, and his six target schools were all ranked in the top twenty. So far, so good. But when I began to ask him some basic questions that I would ask any MBA applicant, I saw that Alex fell into the all-too-familiar trap of focusing on the idea of earning an MBA without focusing on why he wanted it.

---

1   All client names have been changed.

For example, when I asked him, "What is your short-term, post-MBA goal?" he said, "I'm interested in technology entrepreneurship, consulting, or possibly marketing."

"That isn't a goal, Alex. That's a list," I told him. "If you write all of those in a goals essay, or state that in an interview, it will be a loud signal to the admissions committee that you haven't a clue what you want to do. In the best case, you will seem as if you lack focus. At worst, your application will be quickly dismissed. You can't offer a kaleidoscope of goals, or you're going to get dinged."

A goal is something you want to do, not just study

I don't mean to be too hard on Alex. In his mid-twenties, with a lot of talent, energy and an eagerness to explore the untapped potential of his budding career, he understandably wanted to remain open to various possibilities and was just being honest about it. Like many other clients I have worked with, Alex was at first surprised when I told him his goals were too fuzzy. I told him what I have told countless other prospective MBA students: Goals must be credible, clear, and sincere. They must specify not only industry, but function. In fact, well-defined goals are as much a requirement in successful MBA admissions as GMAT, GPA, and work experience. *They are front and center in the minds of admissions readers. Put them front and center in your mind as you prepare to apply.*

Alex was a little bit thrown by this at first. He asked me, "Don't the schools know that even if you have one goal in mind when you apply to MBA programs, your goals might change?"

"Sure they do," I told him. "Nobody knows what the future will bring, Alex, but your choice of an MBA program has to show that you have thoughtfully charted a course that leads from where you have been to where you want to go. A goal has to include the industry you'd like to work in as well as the role or function you want to play in that industry. What do you want to accomplish in this field? What impact do you hope to make? The schools also want to know what motivates you to choose this goal in the first place."

Alex nodded thoughtfully, so I continued.

"There's more. Schools will also want to know that you're a good fit for their program in other respects. You need to honestly assess not only your academic and professional achievements, but also your personality, learning style and preferences for location while in school. Not everybody is cut out for the cold northeast. Not everybody thrives as much in an urban setting as they do in a quieter locale."

"That makes sense. I just hadn't thought about all these things before," Alex admitted.

Alex could have made a mental note not to call me for any further consulting and walked away. Instead, he hired me to work with him and ultimately was accepted at one of his top choice schools.

How Alex defined his goals for his MBA and beyond

Based on my suggestion, Alex began to think more deeply about certain aspects of his personality and experience, some of which he had not at first connected with the work of choosing and applying to business schools. For example, I recommended that he first *look inward* and ask himself the following: *What do I enjoy and where do I excel? What lessons and values can I bring from my nonprofessional life to my professional life?*

Then I recommended he *look outward* and consider what professional paths would take advantage of his strengths and offer the potential to give him more of what he found satisfying.

In addition to these considerations, Alex thought about other personal preferences that could affect his choice of target schools. As part of this process, we brainstormed together about his goals, an exercise that Alex found a little intimidating at first but ultimately liberating. Taking time for deeper self-reflection led Alex to refine those goals in a more targeted fashion, ultimately focusing on technology entrepreneurship. This made the most sense for him not only given his professional experience, but also because he was genuinely more enthusiastic about this option than the other options he had considered in marketing or consulting.

Research – With his newly refined goals and understanding about his own needs, Alex did further research about various programs and their "personalities" to consider where he was really a better fit. This resulted in crossing two schools off his list and replacing them with two others that he hadn't even considered before but whose strengths, recruitment record, location and learning style were excellent matches for him. While the two new programs were outside the top ten, both were excellent programs. His choices also showed me that Alex was willing to look beyond the sometimes blinding star status of the highest-ranked programs to find ones that would still provide an outstanding education and an even better fit – or scholarship money.

Writing with focus – Alex's exercise in refining his goals and values clarification immediately enabled him to write with more confidence and passion about his career path and why he was well-suited for the schools where he ultimately applied. In taking this more deliberate method of choosing schools, he learned something that may sound deceptively simple but is too often forgotten: A goal is something you want to *do*, not just study.

What is your situation?

Some applicants may be very clear about either the industry in which they want to work or the function or job title they'd like to have, but not always both. For example, you may be certain that you want to grow into a marketing executive role but are much less clear about what product or service you'd like to help market. There's an enormous difference in what you will need to know if you choose healthcare marketing versus technology marketing, or entertainment marketing versus automotive marketing, or real estate marketing versus social enterprise marketing. These all fall under the large umbrella of marketing. However, the differences among those industries and the knowledge and skills needed to work within them could lead you to choose among different MBA programs.

Taking the example further, does your career goal in marketing include business development, market research, brand management or channel management? Focusing more sharply on the nuances of your chosen industry or chosen job function can and should affect your school selection.

This doesn't mean your career trajectory has to be completely linear. For example, let's say you are a software consultant who has worked on software marketing projects or a software designer who has worked in product development. Now you now want to go into brand management in the software industry. This goal still makes sense. It is focused and clear. This sort of clarity is a vital asset to you in the application process.

Draw a direct line from where you have been to where you want to go.

As you chart your post-MBA goals, write down the answers to the following questions. This exercise will help you in your own process of clarifying your goals and helping you pinpoint the most suitable schools for you.

- ☑ What aspects of your work **experience** have given you the most satisfaction?

- ☑ Where do you envision your greatest **potential** to grow professionally?

- ☑ What is your driving **motivation** to pursue this goal?

- ☑ What **character traits** do you possess that will be an asset in a given role or industry?

- ☑ When did you first discover an **opportunity** or need in your desired industry or function?

- ☑ What is your long-term **vision** for your career at this point, and how will your short-term goal logically lead to the realization of your long-term career vision?

Your goals will certainly evolve over time, and when you apply to MBA programs you may be genuinely torn between two equally compelling short-term goals. But by the time you sit down to write your goals essay, *you need to draw a direct line from where you have been in your career and where you want to go.*

Later on in the application process you are likely to be asked to discuss both short-term and long-term career goals, so it's useful to think about the distinction between those now. To help you visualize what that path will look like, ask yourself the following questions:

☑   What would your ideal position be at each of these stages?

☑   What specific goals or milestones would you like to achieve at each stage?

☑   What impact would you hope to have on the people you work with and in your chosen field?

☑   What type of company or companies would you work for along the way?

Do your research so that your goals are achievable. If you are not already well-versed in what is happening in your target industry, research hiring trends, services, organization, market status, products and competitive concerns in your field and in the kind of companies you would like to work for, then seek informational interviews with people in the positions you aspire to as well as with recruiters in your target field. These efforts will also help you write intelligently about your chosen field and show that you understand its current needs, challenges and opportunities. And they will help you see where you can make your mark.

What if you're a career changer?

If you are a career changer, then how do you chart your course? The truth is that well over half of all MBA students are career changers, and some schools estimate the figure is closer to 80 or 90 percent if "career changer" is defined as a change in either industry or function. So you will have a lot of company in the applicant pool. Although a majority of MBA applicants are changing careers, you still must present the case that you are sufficiently informed about your new field and role to make it seem a credible, authentic choice for you. Again, research is critical, including interviewing people who already work in the field. Think about what skills you already possess that will be an asset in your new field. Let's say you come from a not-for-profit background and want to go into business consulting. Your skills may already include excellent fundraising, organizational and people-management skills, which can transfer – with help – to business consulting. Applicants from the military often have many traits that are highly desirable in the business world, such as leadership and operations management, even if they have not worked in a business setting.

Remember to have a Plan B

An MBA program that accepts you wants to feel confident that you will be employable at the end of their program. Part of your job in convincing them that you are a good investment is to show them that if your ideal career path takes a circuitous route or doesn't pan out, you are agile enough, smart enough and prepared enough to have a credible Plan B in mind. Our economy has endured several volatile years, and the pace of change in the economy keeps increasing faster and faster, forcing changes in almost every industry. How ready will you be to adapt? Is your vision specific enough to show focus, yet also broad enough to embrace the need to change course if necessary? If you are a career changer or are trying to enter a field where the bar to entry is already very high, such as venture capital or private equity, be prepared with an alternate career route that will eventually get you to your dream goal.

Where do you want to live during school, and where do you want to work after school?

Your career goals and the knowledge and skills that you need from an MBA education remain the primary focus as you target your schools, but don't gloss over other important considerations. For example, an increasing percentage of MBA applicants to U.S. schools are from outside the United States and are passionate about returning to their countries of origin, bringing with them a sophisticated set of business skills that they will apply to enhance an industry or field back home. If this is your situation, look for programs that offer coursework and programs that specialize in doing business in the part of the world where you plan to establish your career, including highly regarded MBA programs abroad.

And speaking of geography, you will likely spend two full years in an MBA program. Where will you be happiest living during that time? Do you want to live in a big city or small college town? Do you prefer a big university or a smaller, more intimate environment? Are you excited by the cultural opportunities of a lively urban center, or would you rather not be distracted and prefer a more rural setting? Your lifestyle, values and budget will also dictate which schools are better matches for you than others. And if you are married or living with a partner, how does your spouse or partner feel about moving to these new locations with you? Will he or she be able to find a job?

13

Curriculum style, clubs, recruitment history, and other considerations

In thinking about your post-MBA goals, you also need to consider several aspects of your target schools that can best support those goals and likely career path. These will all involve looking closely at their curriculum, programs, clubs, recruitment history and financial aid/scholarship possibilities. I'll develop this topic in much more detail in Chapter 2, but for now, keep in mind that each school offers different educational approaches. Before choosing a school, make sure you understand their teaching methodology and flexibility of the curriculum. Does the program have specialty tracks in your field? For applicants with specific goals, this criterion plays a more significant role.

I hope that by now I've convinced you beyond any doubt that taking the time to fine tune your career goals, short term and long term, is an invaluable investment of your time. No matter how busy you are now, you need to take the time for this kind of self-reflection, which will result in applications that show the admissions committee that your goals are carefully considered, informed and appropriate for you. While some of my clients at first balk a little at doing this work, they have all thanked me for it afterward, saying how much clearer and more confident they feel about their applications and their goals.

As Dean Robert Bruner of the Darden School of Business (University of Virginia) once wrote on his blog, "If you don't know where you're going, any road will take you there. As the Proverb says, 'Without a vision, the people will perish.' A big red flag is having no vision for your future. Without a vision, you might as well throw a dart to select a school. Better yet, without a vision you might as well defer your enrollment until you have figured things out."[2]

Once you have your vision, you are better prepared to identify the schools that are the best match for *you*. That's what we will do in the next chapter.

---

2   http://blogs.darden.virginia.edu/deansblog/2007/04/deciding-to-accept-an-offer-of-admission-what-role-should-rankings-play/

The Bottom Line

→ Invest the time and energy to **define your goals** for an MBA education and beyond.

→ **Look inward** to discover what you enjoy and where you excel. Then **look outward** to consider likely professional paths that will maximize your strengths and maximize your chances for professional fulfillment.

→ **Distinguish between short-term and long-term goals** and how you will map your course from where you have been to where you want to go.

→ **Research** the educational approach, curriculum flexibility, specialty tracks, recruitment possibilities, location, financial aid, and even extracurricular clubs and student life at your target schools.

→ Clear, well-defined goals are as much a requirement in successful MBA admissions as GMAT, GPA, and work experience. They are front and center in the minds of admissions readers. **Put goals front and center in your mind as you prepare to apply.**

Chapter 2

How to Research MBA Programs and Why It's Essential That You Do

What schools send the most grads in the direction you want to go?

Now that you have given more thought to your goals for an MBA and your career beyond, you will be much better positioned to determine a list of MBA programs that can help you achieve those goals. This new self-knowledge will make it much easier to figure out which programs offer what you need and want to learn as well as what type of environment (educational, geographic and social) is most complementary to you. I hope that many of you will also be more open to learning about other program gems that you might not have considered, or even heard of, but which might fit you like a custom-tailored suit. In this chapter I'll show you how to do the smart detective work you need to go beneath the surface and feel confident that your MBA matchmaking is really a match!

I'll repeat my guiding philosophy here (borrowed with thanks from Stephen Covey) because I hope it will become your guiding philosophy, too: "Begin with the end in mind." Start your search by visualizing your final destination. What does your career vision look like? Are you standing at the podium at a shareholders' meeting as the CEO of a corporation, fielding questions about company performance? Are you pitching a group of venture capitalists to invest in your new, dazzling technology product? Are you rolling out a bold new marketing campaign for a not-for-profit? Whatever your vision, *you want to find out the most likely path* from MBA to that podium, that boardroom, or that corner office. In other words, you need to find out which MBA schools send the most grads in the direction you want to go.

How useful are the MBA rankings?

One of the most popular ways that applicants look for this information is by consulting the rankings for MBA programs in *U.S. News & World Report* and *Businessweek*. Some applicants view these rankings as no less than divinely revealed Truth filtered down to poor applicants from on high. Big mistake. Let's understand what the rankings are and what they are not. The rankings are surveys and collections of data that provide convenient ways for applicants to compare schools on specific criteria, but the metrics they utilize are fairly superficial. They attempt to measure such qualities as reputation, student stats and GMAT scores, return on investment (ROI) and recruiter satisfaction. Therefore, schools can be ranked with wildly differing results depending on the criteria used.

For example, Duke Fuqua was ranked #6 by *Businessweek* (*BW*) in 2010, #20 in Global MBA Rankings by *The Financial Times* (2011), #12 by *US News* (2011), #13 in *Forbes* (2010), and #18 by *The Economist* (2011). Each list measures different factors and therefore yields different results. If you want to zero in on a specific metric, you can dig deeper and compare schools easily on that metric, provided you have the right ranking. For example, *BW* bases its rankings on employer and student surveys as well as what they call "intellectual capital." If you want to compare what recruiters think of different MBA programs, go to *BW*. *The Financial Times* factors in diversity and international reach, alumni salaries and career development, and research capabilities. *Forbes'* top ten is determined primarily by ROI measurements, reported by graduates from six years earlier. *U.S. News* also allows you to rank or select programs by a limited set of criteria, such as admissions stats, school specialties, tuition or class size. If you want to know what students thought of their MBA experience, turn to *BW* and *The Economist's* "Which MBA" section. Plan to study in Europe? Check the ranking of European programs in *The Financial Times*.

Now consider what the rankings are *not*: They are not objective measures of educational quality that apply across the board to all students. Nothing can fit that bill. Educational quality is highly subjective and experts debate it endlessly. While specialty rankings do provide valuable focus for specific fields, student objectives still vary widely, so "quality" differs from student to student. Again, your individual criteria should be determinative. For example, a female student interested in strategy consulting wants to attend a business school with a strong women's network. She is interested in the surveys conducted by *US News* and *Businessweek* on leading schools in general management. In addition, *The Financial Times* allows her to rank schools based on the percentage of women in class and on faculty. However, no single ranking replicates her criteria exactly. Furthermore, her decisive factors differ markedly from that of a married male applicant who prefers an urban school so his wife can find work more easily and who wants to go into portfolio management.

Rankings are best used to help you determine particular preferences and values of a school. They can be the launching pad for your school research, not the final destination.

At best, the data compiled help you rank programs according to *your* values, preferences, and criteria, while taking into account your qualifications, goals, and personal preferences. But the rankings are also leveraged to create excitement and sell magazines. And because they succeed in creating this excitement, they also are often misused or used as a substitute for real, boots-on-the-ground research. This buzz can lull applicants into a false sense that they have done their research just by checking the rankings instead of truly investigating program distinctions, strengths and weaknesses. In such cases, applicants can make a potentially costly mistake and end up applying to or attending the wrong program. Learn to be a savvy investor in your MBA education. Remember that rankings, especially those that have a survey component, are proxies for reputation and brand, but reputation is not the same as quality and fit. Know the difference. As Robert Bruner, Dean of the Darden School of Business, wrote on his blog[3], "Friends don't let friends accept admission just on the basis of rankings."

When you do refer to the rankings, keep in mind their very real limitations:

 1.   *Variability.* They don't measure exactly what's important to you.

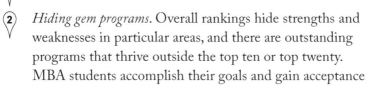 2.   *Hiding gem programs.* Overall rankings hide strengths and weaknesses in particular areas, and there are outstanding programs that thrive outside the top ten or top twenty. MBA students accomplish their goals and gain acceptance

---

3   http://blogs.darden.virginia.edu/deansblog/2007/04/deciding-to-accept-an-offer-of-admission-what-role-should-rankings-play/

or have a better chance of obtaining financial aid when they recognize those gems.

(3) *The problem of averages.* Averages aren't a cutoff and don't reflect extenuating circumstances or the interplay between myriad factors in an admissions decision. Applicants are accepted with below average stats and are rejected with above average stats.

(4) *Surveys can be gamed.* This is especially true of surveys of students and alumni (*Businessweek, Financial Times, The Economist*), who understand that higher rankings increase the value of their degrees and have an incentive to think kindly of their schools.

(5) *Lack of information.* Survey respondents are not always well informed. They don't necessarily know about recent developments and new programs at the schools they are ranking. They are opining based on what they experienced years ago or "heard."

(6) *Valuing "so what?" factors.* For those rankings that survey recruiters (*Businessweek*), realize that recruiters may value factors that you couldn't care less about. Does a school's offering good service for recruiters, excellent MBAs willing to work for low pay, and comfortable interview rooms really matter in your selection of an MBA program?

(7) *Lack of nuance.* The raw rankings don't reveal the degree of difference among schools. For example, there could be a real difference in international or even national opportunity in a program ranked 25th as opposed to 5th. There is probably little difference in overall opportunity for a program ranked 8th as opposed to 13th.

(8) *Varying measurements of ROI.* Return on investment measures may reflect geographic differences or differences in starting salaries in particular industries more than educational quality.

Rankings are a good place to begin school research and an absolutely terrible place to end it. In addition to the limitations listed above, the rankings frequently mirror commonly held beliefs about institutions. Reputation and brand can play a role in your application and acceptance decisions, but they should never be the primary reason you apply for or accept an offer of admission. After you research a school's strengths and weaknesses, educational approach, culture, admitted student profiles, and educational and professional opportunities, then you can consider brand.

Who's hiring at your target schools?

After you've reviewed the rankings with these caveats in mind, you'll want to uncover critical information that many applicants don't think about early enough in the game: Who is hiring from your target programs? Tracking down this information is the next logical step to determining which schools are steering grads in the direction you want to go. Many MBA programs offer extensive information on recruitment and hiring directly on their websites. Some have full employment reports with helpful pie charts that you can click to directly or else download instantly. These reports can be extremely thorough in breaking down information very completely, including:

- ☑ Rosters of recruiting companies
  (sometimes broken down by year)

- ☑ Numbers of grads hired
  (in percentages of the class and raw numbers)

- ☑ Hiring stats by industry, function, and location

- ☑ Internship data

- ☑ Salary averages

- ☑ Actual source of job
  (alumni contact, internship, interview, etc.)

When school websites don't offer this information online, call the career services office and ask for it. And speaking of career services, find out how extensive those services are and what you can look forward to. These services are also often listed on the websites, and will vary widely. They may include a few or many of the following:

☑ Career classes that help coach you through the interviewing and salary negotiation process

☑ Peer counseling from seasoned second-year students

☑ One-on-one coaching with staff who are knowledgeable about current trends in your field

☑ Career club workshops

☑ Alumni mentor programs

☑ Job search luncheons

☑ Mock interviews

☑ Resume reviews

☑ Industry panel events

Schools have a vested interest in your success and do their best to prepare you for that outcome. As part of your research, it will be good to know what's on the menu in career counseling services at the schools of your choice.

Networking, clubs and events, oh my!

While career services are obviously critical, they are not the exclusive transportation to your post-MBA goal. Two other elements of b-school life will also provide the means to your objective: The in-class and extracurricular activities. As you research your schools, make sure you understand how these aspects of the programs will help you achieve your goals. What about the experiential opportunities works for you? Which extracurricular activities are professionally valuable or just appeal to you on a personal level? What networking opportunities exist? What clubs and events connect to your future?

Make note of the relevant curricular and extracurricular elements that appeal because those notes will be critical when you start writing your essays and presenting your reasons for applying to Dream B-School.

While professional opportunities should clearly be your top priority, they are not the only factors you should weigh. Here are several others in a suggested order of importance, but your order may vary:

1. *Educational methodology.* Do you prefer a mix of methodologies? Check out Wharton. Do you seek an emphasis on projects and hands-on learning, like they offer at Ross? Do you want strict case method? Take a closer look at HBS and Darden.

2. *Clubs and extracurriculars.* Many schools have imitated MIT Sloan's business plan competition, but not everyone has a social enterprise competition (HBS does). If you are interested in social enterprise, that competition may be particularly appealing. What are some of the unusual clubs at the different schools that might interest you? For example, almost every school will have a marketing club, but only some, like Columbia, will have a luxury goods marketing club. Again, if this is your interest, the existence and strength of that club may be an important attraction for you.

3. *The class profile.* Do you want a large class or a small, close-knit class? Do you want an urban or rural setting? Do you really want to be in a class that draws over 70 percent of its students from engineering, business, and technical fields? Or would you prefer to be in a class where 46 percent came from the social sciences and humanities? Both MIT and Stanford provide outstanding MBA educations, but their classes are comprised very differently. You may prefer one or the other.

Now that you know what you're looking for, it's time to start doing your homework.

Why campus visits are a good idea

You live in Denver, but your top choice programs are Haas and Columbia. Do you really need to crisscross the country for school visits? And what about a visit to Kenan-Flagler in Chapel Hill, which you consider a strong second choice? How much traveling can you afford, in time, money and missed work? The cost-benefit analysis is something you have to do individually, but here's the scoop on school visits.

Some admissions directors, particularly if representing smaller schools outside of urban areas, have made it clear that they value visits and take them as signs of interest, especially for domestic or local applicants. At the same time, directors at Harvard, Wharton, Stanford and other top schools have stated unequivocally that they do not weigh a campus visit as a factor in an admissions decision. And certainly outstanding candidates would never be denied entry on the basis of not having visited the school.

But do any of these statements mean that campus visits to target schools, even those schools that say they don't "count" visits, are a waste of time and effort? On the contrary!

Schools may not officially award "brownie points" for visiting, but a campus visit can only increase your chances of acceptances--not because of imaginary points bestowed--but *because you will be a better informed applicant.* Having sat in on a class or two, had coffee with students, seen where you might live, walked around campus, and observed and listened, you will have a tangible feel for the program and its personality. You will have a better feel for how well it supports your goals. If the visit fulfills your expectations, you'll be able to answer the "Why Our School?" part of the essay with specificity and confidence, based on a true story. If you are fortunate enough to be able to visit two schools, each of which you find equally compelling beforehand, one is almost sure to rise to the top of your list after those visits. Wouldn't it be great to know where you really fit and where you don't?

Do your homework before you arrive

If you can swing a campus visit and the guilt over the additional global warming won't give you night terrors, be smart about scheduling your trip. Consult the school's virtual Chamber of Commerce – its website. Read as much as you can so that you arrive as well-informed as possible. You won't make a fabulous impression by asking a question on campus that is answered in three different places on the website. At the same time, reading content on the website should also trigger questions for you to ask during your visit. Write down your questions and bring them with you. And since you never know whom you might meet or have an opportunity to talk to when you are on campus, be prepared to state with confidence your short-term career goals and why you are attracted to this program.

You'll also want to check the school's events calendar to see when they offer campus tours and other informational sessions for applicants. That quick check will prevent the mistake of arriving the week before final exams, when only the most saintly students will take the time to speak to you. Some applicants try to combine campus visits with vacations, but that's a bad idea if you choose early December: The admissions staff will be up to their ears reading applications and have no time to answer your questions, and students will be taking off for their own school breaks.

If you are planning to apply during Round 1, it would be ideal to visit during the spring semester beforehand. If you wait till the fall you risk being overwhelmed by the tasks of juggling your work schedule (and making up for missed days), completing your applications carefully and thoughtfully, as well as traveling. Additionally, first-year students who have really just arrived will have less of substance to tell you compared to the spring, when they are more seasoned. Let the school know that you are planning your visit and introduce yourself when you are there. Dress in casual business attire unless you have an interview scheduled, when you'll want to dress more formally.

Then take a tour, participate in an information session, and sit in on a class or two. Remember that if you are sitting in on a class, you are there to listen and observe, not to participate. Take advantage of whatever is offered but don't feel constrained by the organized activities alone. Introduce yourself to students. Try to find those who have career interests similar to you. Invite them for lunch or coffee and hear what they have to say about the program. Naturally, the questions you ask when on campus will be guided by your particular interests, but here are some general questions I recommend when visiting schools:

- ☑ What is a typical day like for a first-year or second-year student?

- ☑ Do professors teach an integrated approach to business, one that emphasizes the interconnection of business functions?

Or are they teaching their specific class without a larger framework? If it is interconnected, how do they coordinate with other professors?

☑ How do professors balance teaching and research?

☑ How are interview slots assigned? Is there bidding process? What is it?

Do not ask questions that will seem self-absorbed and silly, such as, What do you think my chances are of getting in? These will quickly become annoying and reveal that you are governed more by insecurity rather than genuine curiosity about the program.

Finally, after your campus visit, ask yourself the most important question of all: *Can I see myself here?*

How to pay an effective "virtual" school visit

I realize that for many, if not most applicants (particularly international applicants applying to U.S. schools), a school visit is simply out of the question. Don't worry. There are many valuable channels that can yield the information you need to make an informed decision about where to apply, and to help you when answering a frequently asked essay/interview question, "What steps have you taken to learn about Our Amazing MBA Program?"

First, you can attend school-sponsored receptions and information sessions either in your city or another one within reasonable traveling distance. The same questions that you gathered from studying the website can still be asked at these sessions. Schools also often participate in larger MBA fairs organized during the fall and held in many major cities across the world. How can you get the most out of attending these fairs? Peter von Loesecke, CEO and Managing Director of The MBA Tour LLC (thembatour.com), which organizes information sessions between MBA admissions representatives and prospective students, offers these tips[4]:

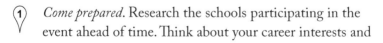 *Come prepared.* Research the schools participating in the event ahead of time. Think about your career interests and

---

4   Excerpted from an interview with Linda Abraham and posted in a blog post called The MBA Tour (http://blog.accepted.com/acceptedcom_blog/2009/7/28/the-mba-tour-qa.html)

goals and know how an MBA helps you achieve those goals and interests.

(2) *Make a good impression.* Have your resume available and wear business attire. Business casual is ok, but most serious students, especially those outside the United States, attend in business attire. Ask questions that pertain to your personal situation and goals, and asking questions that can be answered off the school's internet site. Don't monopolize conversations with school reps; limit your chats to between three and five minutes unless no one else is waiting.

(3) *Expand your horizons. Don't be limited by first impressions of programs and where you want to go to school. Try and visit as many schools as you can and have your visit recorded so there is a record of interest at that program.*

(4) *Ask for business cards.* This way you can send follow-up emails thanking them for the time they spent with you. You can even resend your resume too!

(5) *Don't ask questions that are not relevant to your situation or that show you haven't done any research.*
Questions not to ask include:

- ☑ *"What is your average GMAT score?"* Research this online on *Businessweek* or through other sources.

- ☑ *"Tell me why I should apply to your school."* This sort of question implies you think the school would be privileged to accept you and shows arrogance.

- ☑ *"Where is your school located?"* Another question that reveals no prior research.

- ☑ *"How strong are your career services in this city?"* A better question is: *"Does your career services center have connections into XYZ industry where I am looking for a position after graduation?"* The second question is a fair question and should be asked. The first one will generate a predictable response of "Of course we are strong in job placement in this city."

If you still can't get to a school or visit a school fair…

You can amass a wealth of information without even leaving your chair or couch thanks to the internet. Blogs, articles, podcasts, videocasts, chat transcripts, and other information are available through individual school websites, my company's (Accepted.com), and others such as businessweek.com/bschools, mbapodcaster.com, worldmbatour.com, poetsandquants.com and thembatour.com. These resources will provide valuable insights and help you learn in-depth about the programs you are interested in and enable you to narrow down your search.

Revisit your target list of schools after your preliminary research

As your enthusiasm builds for certain programs, revisit their websites to see how they present themselves. At first glance, many of the programs will market themselves using similar phrases and words: They promise to give their students an "edge," with a "globally recognized degree." They'll teach "highly valued leadership skills" in a "rigorous" program. You can bet they'll boast of their "world-class faculty" who will provide "open-door access." Oh yes, there will be a "supportive alumni network," and I'll bet my mother's heirloom sapphire and diamond pendant they'll also promise a "tight-knit, collaborative community." Much of this may be true. In some cases, it all may be true, but that only underscores how important it is to dig deeper to determine how well the program will fit your personality and goals. Look at their curriculum, including other options for an advanced business education outside the classic two-year, full-time MBA program. Given your recent reevaluation of your career goals and experience, are you still certain that the classic, two-year MBA program is right for you? Is it possible that another advanced business degree program would suit you better, such as a master's of real estate business development (Columbia); a master's of management in healthcare (Vanderbilt); a dual-degree program that combines an MBA with a JD, or an MBA with a master's of engineering (Kellogg)?

Spend time reviewing what the faculty is teaching and studying as well, with an eye toward instructors who specialize in your area of interest. Do you spot instructors who have written a business book that has become your bible? Instructors who are actively researching or consulting on projects in your area of interest? Professors whose work and industry contributions you have long admired? Are these and other professors teaching what you need to learn to fill the gaps in your knowledge and skill sets?

Is your knowledge current?

Don't assume that because one of your best friends graduated from one of your target programs three years ago and told you all about it that you are sufficiently informed about the curriculum. MBA programs frequently revise their curricula to stay current with trends in business and business education. The changes may not be dramatic, but the tweaks and new emphases may be enough to give you pause or to make you even more excited about the school. For example, some programs have introduced a more liberal arts approach to business, while others have tried to add muscle to their leadership curriculum. In 2011, even Harvard Business School, which has staked its preeminent brand for decades on the case method, introduced a required experiential "field immersion experience" as well as greater flexibility in its elective offerings. Make sure your knowledge of the program is this year's, not last year's, before settling on target schools.

One of your best sources of current information will be other MBA applicants, students and alumni. Not surprisingly, enterprising MBA alum (Wharton, '06) created a clearinghouse of sorts for student blogs called hella (hella. opencoder.org), which is a portal to musings from current MBA students and recent grads. You might also happen upon interviews with MBA professors, tips on networking and looking for internships, and more. In addition to student blogs, some MBA programs also have student newspapers and/or online publications. Look them up for more insights into what your potential student colleagues are saying and thinking.

Adding the personal touch to networking

Networking and conducting informational interviews can also help you clarify your best school picks as well as shine a light on how you can enter or advance in your field of choice. Try to find current students and alumni from your target schools as well as potential employers and others who have "boots on the ground" in your chosen career. Their insights can help you further refine your roadmap for career advancement. And you can ask current students about the things they like best and dislike most about their program.

If you are interviewing alumni, ask them: What did you find most valuable in your MBA program? What advice do you have about tailoring an MBA curriculum to suit the current and emerging needs of this industry? If you are interviewing someone who works at the kind of company--if not *the* company--where you'd love to work, ask them: What skills and traits does this company value most in the role I hope to win? If you can score an interview with potential employers, make it clear from the start that you are not asking for a job, just for brief advice on how best to continue mapping out your plan for career advancement. What advice do they have on how an advanced business degree will help you achieve your short-term career milestones? If your personal networking doesn't yield enough interview prospects, use other networking resources, such as LinkedIn or Facebook, professional organizations, and perhaps the alumni associations of the MBA programs you like best.

In summary, on your road to acceptance at the right MBA program for you, you'll want to do all the following:

- ☑ Scour the schools' websites for information about student body, academics and recruitment.

- ☑ Visit the schools if possible, and/or attend receptions and informational events hosted by the schools.

- ☑ Participate in third-party events, such as in-person and virtual MBA fairs, and Accepted's online Q&As.

- ☑ Regularly visit or subscribe to sites including *Businessweek's* MBA section, *Poets and Quants*, and *MBA50*.

- ☑ Talk to current students and/or recent alumni.

- ☑ Read hella.opencoder.org's student blogs to get a feel for campus life.

Understanding the differences among business schools takes time but is extremely worthwhile. Grasping these points of difference will enable you to make more intelligent application and acceptance decisions.

In the next chapter, I'll show you how to assess your qualifications for the schools you now know you are interested in.

The Bottom Line

→ **Understand the limitations of MBA rankings.** Use them to determine particular preferences and values of a school, but know that differing criteria used result in wildly differing results.

→ **Investigate the available career services,** such as mentoring programs, resume review, and career workshops, at the schools you are investigating and **research recruiting and hiring data** as well. Make sure that schools you apply send grads in the direction you want to go.

→ **Research both in-class and extra-curricular activities** such as clubs and networking opportunities to understand how the program will help you achieve your goals.

→ **Plan campus visits if possible.** Time your visits so you can sit in on classes, meet students, and get a feel for campus life. Otherwise, **attend school-sponsored information sessions** or larger MBA fairs near you.

→ **Interview people working in your field and/or current students and alumni** of your target schools. They can offer further advice and insights on achieving your career goals.

How Qualified Are You?

The numbers don't always tell the whole story.
But they still matter.

In the last chapter I showed you how to dig for the information you need on your target schools to make an informed decision. After all, your goal is not only to gain acceptances in general; you are out to gain acceptances at the specific programs that can help you turn your career dream into reality. Once you have determined the best schools for you, the question then becomes, Are you good enough for them? In this chapter I'll show you how to figure out if you have what it takes to earn an acceptance at your top-choice schools.

When MBA programs are deciding whether to admit you, they are going to evaluate the following:

- ☑ Intellectual horsepower – proving you can do a regression analysis without fainting

- ☑ Professional savvy and acumen – work experience matters

- ☑ Personal qualities valued by your target programs – leadership and other desirable qualities

- ☑ Why admit *you?* Diversity is more than race and gender

How are these qualities evaluated?

Let's start with *intellectual horsepower*. For competitive MBA programs and in the large business world beyond, you'll have to prove that you can crunch numbers like a pro. The main litmus test for these quant skills has long been the Graduate Management Admission Test, the GMAT. For decades, this test has proven a nearly fail-safe predictor of success for first-year MBA students. It is also the only common denominator among all MBA students, except for those taking the GRE. More on that a bit later.

To see if your GMAT score is competitive for your target schools, check each school's website to find out the average GMAT scores of their students. For a top ten or top fifteen program, you'll want to score in the 80th percentile on both quant and verbal, which will yield a robust 700 or higher overall.

That said, your abilities should appear to be fairly balanced. If you scored in the 95th percentile in the quant section but only 56th in the verbal, for example, your overall score may still be competitive but you'll be off kilter. Strong MBA candidates must also have effective communication skills. After all, how can you be an effective business leader if you are not an effective communicator? While well-written essays are a must, and professional editing can help you achieve them, it will seem suspicious if you show up for an interview with English skills that don't match the fluency of your essays. If you need help with your writing skills, enroll in a writing class to burnish them. You can also find courses geared toward business writing at a local community college, university extension, or online. Whenever possible, choose a course that is more than just a day-long seminar, which would have limited impact.

While I have emphasized that MBA programs are looking for fit, and view you as a multifaceted individual, there's no getting around the fact that a low GMAT score (close to and below the bottom of the school's 80 percent range) will hurt your candidacy. The good news is that it isn't necessarily a deal breaker. Like GPAs, these scores are viewed in the context of your entire profile. Try to interpret your scores as a member of the admissions committee: Is the rest of your profile stellar? Do you have solid grades in quant-related courses? Is it possible that you're just not great at standardized tests? Is your score not so low relative to other applicants in your demographic group? Are you applying to schools where the average GMAT score is within reasonable distance from your lower-than-you-would have-wished score?

If you conclude your score is low and you think you can raise it, you should prepare for and retake the GMAT. If your practice scores were significantly higher than the real thing, if you were sick on test day, or there was an earthquake in the middle of your exam, you probably could do better. While I can imagine that you would rather have your molars extracted (at least your mouth is anesthetized) than retake the GMAT, a do-over after additional study could boost your score and your competitiveness.

Can you do a regression analysis without fainting?

But if you get a disappointing quant score that will not be balanced by any other demonstrations of your quant skills (such as an A-average as an undergrad or highly quantitative work), and you don't believe you can raise your GMAT, you will have to take other action. Enroll in a calculus, statistics and/or accounting class at your local community college--ASAP. Make sure you have the prerequisite skills; you will need to earn an A! If you have time, take additional quant-oriented courses, such as finance or economics. Sometimes you can find quant classes designed specifically for aspirants to MBA programs, which might have titles like "Mathematics for Management" or "Business Applications for Calculus." Other evidence of quant skills would include obtaining a Chartered Financial Analyst (CFA) or similar certification. Particularly if you are a "poet," someone from a liberal arts background, laying a better foundation for the quant work that will be expected of you will help your chances immeasurably.

These extra classes and programs will also help you create an alternative transcript that can amend, if not supersede, your original college transcript by showing all the supplemental quant work you have performed. Needless to say, you will have to earn excellent grades in these supplemental classes to be competitive at any well-regarded MBA program.

If your quant grades and GMAT scores are only lackluster but you've done impressive work with numbers on the job, you will have to highlight these quantitative achievements in your essays. Use vivid details, examples, and anecdotes that will prove to the adcoms that your low quant score was really a fluke and that it's clear that there are no quant problems here. Building your case, ask your recommenders to mention specific quantitative achievements in their assessments of you and your work. Having a respected third party vouch for your skills will help you immensely.

If you are retaking the GMAT, invest in one of the excellent GMAT preparation courses available. If you dread the prospect of sitting alone with a GMAT prep book, these courses could make the entire process easier, faster and more effective. These prep courses, either alone or in conjunction with the suggested quant classes, should really push your numbers up. And the good news is that most schools "count" your highest score.

GREs: Catching up to GMAT?

While the GMAT remains the standard test for MBA admissions, there is also a growing acceptance among b-schools of the GRE. An article in the May 10, 2010 issue of *U.S. News & World Report* notes that what began as a trend among a few elite schools has exploded into an almost standard option available at 27 percent of the *U.S. News & World Reports'* 433 b-schools on the *Best Business School* rankings report. More than 600 b-schools as of July 2011, including Stanford, Yale, Harvard, MIT, Stern, Duke and Darden now accept the GRE as an alternative standardized test.[5] Other schools that don't officially accept GREs have also been known to quietly accept them on a case-by-case basis.

Applicants whose quant scores trend on the lower side for MBA programs may be cheered by this news, since GRE math is known to be a bit easier than GMAT math. The added flexibility to take GREs at many programs is also good news for applicants who are applying to dual-degree or additional master's programs that require the test, such as in public policy or economics. Schools also can greatly expand the diversity and size of their applicant pool by accepting the GRE, since more than 600,000 people take the GRE every year compared to only 270,000 taking the GMAT. While some adcom members have stated publicly that they are equally open to applicants submitting GREs as opposed to GMATs, privately many others say that the GMAT remains the gold standard to help determine an applicant's ability to handle the quant work in a rigorous MBA program. This means that your GRE score would have to be even higher to compensate for possible adcom bias in interpreting GRE scores. Unless you feel that your GREs will outshine your expected GMAT quant score by a wide mile, stick with the GMAT. If you do take the GRE and the program's website does not include their score criteria, you may want to call the admissions office to find out what they consider competitive GRE scores.

The other number you will likely be concerned with is your GPA. Like the GMAT or GRE score, your GPA is an important barometer not only of your intelligence, but your ability to apply yourself and succeed in an academic setting. Here too, the numbers don't always tell the whole story. Just as a low GMAT score might only reveal that the test taker had a bad case of nerves or was recovering from flu, a GPA can often undervalue a candidate's true academic potential. For example, many undergraduates' final GPAs are per-

---

5   http://www.ets.org/gre/news/gre_scores_mba_growing

manently depressed because of one poor semester or even a year, after which their performance dramatically improved. Sometimes ill health or other personal difficulties make it impossible to study to full capacity during a segment of your undergraduate years. More often, though, young college students are just too busy partying, swept up in the heady excitement of their first foray into life away from the watchful eyes of mom and dad. Whether they are majoring in fun that first year or spending too much time on extracurricular activities, they often wake up and smell the latte when they face a sobering semester GPA of 2.9. Yes, damage has been done, but students who hunker down and stay serious during the rest of college will have the satisfaction of watching that GPA steadily rise. A slow but steady upward tick in GPA is nothing to worry about; a downward trend is.

Proving you are more qualified than your GPA suggests

There are several ways to show the adcom that you are a better bet than your GPA might suggest. For example, let's say your overall GPA is a 3.2, but you majored in economics and pulled a 3.8 in all your major coursework. Highlighting this important detail will prove you can handle quant material and apply yourself in business-related courses. Of course, this approach only works if you majored in a quant-oriented subject, but I've seen many cases where isolating this part of the GPA really casts an individual's quant skills in a much more flattering light. You can also write a brief optional essay to help explain why a family emergency, illness or even admitted immaturity during your freshman or sophomore year was the culprit behind your 2.9 GPA. If you can demonstrate that after that difficult or immature period ended your GPA during the last two or three years was a steady 3.7, your candidacy will get a boost.

But let's say that despite your best efforts you still completed your college degree with a GPA under 3.0. If you are aiming at an MBA program where the average GPA is 3.5, your chances of acceptance are probably slim. On the other hand, if you apply to a b-school with a GPA average of 3.2, then you have a fighting chance provided the rest of your application is above average.

GPAs will also be weighted differently depending on demographics. For example, Indian engineers or investment bankers from overrepresented ethnicities will have a harder time getting into top MBA programs than a corporate finance executive from an underrepresented background with the same stats. In such a case, a GMAT score in the lower part of the school's 80% range and a GPA of 3.3 may be just too low for one person and just high enough for another.

To recap, if you have a lower-than-ideal GMAT and GPA, here's what you should do:

YOUR CHALLENGE	YOUR ACTION OPTIONS
Initial low GPA that improved through college	1. Discuss what contributed to the low grades either in an optional essay or in a relevant required essay. 2. Point to the improvement as well as to your GMAT score.
Low GMAT Verbal	1. Retake the GMAT. 2. Write compelling essays that prove your strong writing and communication skills. 3. Interview well. 4. Take a course in writing for business. 5. Ask recommenders to comment positively on verbal skills.
Low GMAT quant score	1. Retake the GMAT. 2. Point to other evidence of quantitative ability, such as above average grades in quant classes, demanding work, rigorous professional designations like the CFA, CPA, or FSA. 3. Earn A's in classes like accounting, statistics for business, or calculus if you haven't had them or didn't do well in them. Do NOT take a class you can't do well in. 4. Ask your recommenders to give specific evidence of your quantitative abilities. 5. Highlight quant achievements in job history.
Below average overall GPA	1. Create an alternative transcript with mostly A's in business related classes like accounting, economics, and statistics. 2. In an optional essay, discuss the extenuating circumstances that contributed to the GPA issue and that no longer exist. Or take responsibility for poor time management and immaturity and provide evidence that those qualities are history.
Below average score and GPA	1. Apply to schools where your stats are average or above average. 2. Take several of the steps outlined above to deal with a low GMAT score and academic history so that you effectively improve the academic aspect of your profile.

How work experience shows you're a real grown-up

Even if your GPA and GMAT (or GRE) scores are spectacular, your work experience and personal characteristics still need to impress the admissions readers. Let's first talk about why work experience is so important and what it can reveal about you. Most applicants for two-year, full-time MBA programs have from two to eight years of work experience. If you have been working longer than that, you probably should consider an Executive MBA or other program geared for the more seasoned professional. Unless a program actively courts younger applicants, such as Chicago Booth or CMU Tepper, two years of work experience is usually the effective minimum you will need to prove that you can contribute to and benefit from the program.

Post-college employment reveals that you have "grown-up" experience in taking direction, meeting deadlines and working in teams. These are all highly relevant in a program where group projects are the norm. Developing a baseline track record in your field also gives you industry knowledge and the ability to contribute your insights to class discussions. Finally, recruiters prefer MBAs with work experience.

It isn't only the *quantity* of work experience that is significant – it's the ability to show *how much you have contributed and what impact you have had*. If you have the focus, determination, stick-to-itiveness, collegiality, initiative and maturity that MBA programs prize, chances are you will have found an opportunity to have an impact on the job by applying those skills and traits. And this is true no matter what sort of role you performed, or whether you worked in a large company or fledgling start-up.

For example, if you worked for a large company, such as Infosys, Google, Goldman Sachs, or Bloomberg Financial, the adcoms will understand that you were a small fish in a large pond. They will appreciate that you had to work harder to stand out, but they will also look for signs that you *did*. Advancement in large companies is often highly structured, bureaucratic, and possibly slow, with less room to dazzle supervisors with distinctive skills and abilities. The schools are familiar with the typical path, and if your talents were recognized in such a large organization and you were given a project normally given to someone above your pay grade, or fast-tracked for a promotion, this will add stature to your application. Additionally, the fact that a large company with a valued brand name hired you in the first place is another indication that you probably have at least some of what your MBA program is looking for.

On the other hand, if you joined a start-up or launched an entrepreneurial venture, you will have the opportunity to show how you survived, and perhaps even thrived in those risky, exciting, uncharted waters. In a small company you would have had more occasions to display your adaptability and versatility. You may also have handled more responsibility with less supervision. Most of my clients who joined start-ups or launched entrepreneurial ventures have learned invaluable lessons on a faster track than if they had worked in established firms and wouldn't trade those experiences for anything, even if their entrepreneurial ventures were short lived. Not only did they have to toggle among many disparate kinds of tasks, ranging from sales to public relations to product design, but they also learned – sometimes the hard way – fundamental rules of business planning and formation. If you write about being an entrepreneur, however, you will have to demonstrate that this was not a euphemism for "unemployed." Your business may or may not have succeeded, but showing how you planned and executed it will speak volumes about you. It will show how you strategized, how you determined the need in the market for your product or service, and the logical sequence you applied in launching and managing your enterprise.

The kind of work experience you have had and your career progression helps the adcoms get to know you better. Furthermore, even two years of full-time, professional employment can lend credibility and substance to your stated career goals. They will not be based on a youthful, fuzzy, naive dream, but on some real-world business experience that has tested and refined those goals, clarified where you are heading, and how you will get there. Finally, work experience puts you at a competitive advantage to snag the best jobs after earning your MBA. Think about it. Who is more likely to score those higher paying jobs: the MBA grad with only a year's work experience? Or the one with five years' experience?

Personal qualities valued by your target programs

Competitive MBA programs value more than work experience. They value a range of personal character traits and skills that they look for as you present yourself in your essays and in interviews. The most important among them are *leadership, teamwork, integrity, analytical ability, initiative, organizational ability and communication skills.* Usually, examples of good leadership and teamwork will also encompass other traits as well. However, you may not have had the opportunity to demonstrate all of these highly prized traits and skills on the job. Let's talk about how you can highlight them, either on the job or elsewhere.

Leadership

This is probably the single most important attribute you will need to establish through your application. What can you show the adcoms that will assure them that you a leader capable of running a company, launching a new venture, persuading investors to bet on your new product, and managing employees? Applicants often fail to appreciate how critical it is to show strong leadership experience and potential. I have seen innumerable essay drafts that vaguely mention that applicants have "led a team," without going into any relevant specifics. How many members were on the team? Two? Twelve? Twenty? How long did the team-leading engagement last? What were some of the most significant challenges of that leadership task? What was at stake in the project? Trust me: Inquiring minds on the adcoms will want to know.

Some applicants' professional experiences naturally allowed for significant leadership. Military applicants have often had experience leading groups, often in life-and-death situations. Applicants with several years at tech-based companies often have been tapped to lead cross-functional teams that may have spanned several continents and comprised upwards of twenty people. But even if you have not had significant leadership responsibility on the job, you probably have assumed some leadership roles on sports teams, a drama group, a community service organization, or even within your own family. Below are a few examples that illustrate creative, perceptive and sensitive leadership in non-work settings. I've also highlighted some of the other desirable traits that applicants applied in the context of these leadership initiatives:

HAL - During college, **Hal organized a job fair on campus** along with three other committee members. There was no hierarchy of roles on the committee, but two of the other members really did not get along. Their personality conflicts and disagreements about how the job fair should be planned put the entire project at risk, potentially creating a huge embarrassment and major disappointment to students. Hal took the initiative to speak to each of the warring parties separately and helped them find common ground, managing to snatch job fair victory from the jaws of defeat. In fact, the job fair turned out to be one of the most successful ever at that campus.

This example illustrates many things at once. First, it shows that you can prove leadership experience and potential even when few people are involved. Second, Hal demonstrated **initiative, teamwork, communication, organizational skills** and **analytical abilities** as he navigated among the warring personalities and worked to save an important project.

KURT - **As the captain of a weekend soccer team** comprised of players from more than half a dozen different countries, Kurt had to get players to work together, despite radically divergent playing styles and approaches to practice that stemmed mostly from cultural differences. Initially, practices were frustrating and ineffective, attitudes began to sour, and the team was in last place by mid-season. Kurt's leadership was proven through his **taking initiative, communicating effectively and building teamwork** helped the team come from behind and actually win their division championship by the end of the season.

HARI - Volunteer or other community service activities often provide great leadership opportunities. **Hari joined a community group that desperately needed an overhaul.** The group was dedicated to promoting cultural events but was disorganized, and membership was plummeting. Hari suggested innovative programming ideas, tech-savvy marketing and enhanced membership benefits to the board of directors, which led to his eventual election to president of the organization. Hari **used initiative, communication skills, organizational abilities** and **teamwork** to achieve his tangible success in improving the fortunes of the organization.

JACQUELINE - Finally, **Jacqueline mediated a family battle over succession of a family business.** Her five siblings fought for control of the family business after their mother passed away, and Jacqueline navigated an intensely sensitive situation where emotions ran hot and a multimillion dollar business was at risk of becoming mired in litigation. Jacqueline's ability to earn everyone's trust, patiently coax cooperation, and get everyone to agree to work with a mediator helped reestablish control of the business according to the late matriarch's wishes and smooth the path of succession. This is another example of leadership where the number of people involved was very small, yet the stakes of the leadership initiative were extremely high. Jacqueline's leadership involved skillful use of **initiative, teamwork, communication skills** and **analytical abilities**.

Analytical ability

Can you think through a problem with clarity and foresight? Can you pick apart why a project is lagging, a financial report doesn't match the one you devised, or market share is dropping for your product? The ability to show analytical thinking will burnish your credentials as MBA material. It is also linked to leadership, since your sharp analysis of what is wrong with a project and how to fix it isn't going to do anybody any good if you keep it to yourself. Figuring out a better way to get something done or identifying a significant problem is only half the battle: Once you've run your metrics, studied the competition, and performed your other analyses, you'll need to communicate your results and suggestions to colleagues or supervisors. And they may be resistant to a new way of doing things, or to *your* way of doing things.

Teamwork

Teamwork is a close cousin to leadership and involves many of the same skills. I believe that the essence of teamwork is leadership -- knowing when to lead and when to take a back seat when others on the team are more qualified to be top dog. The examples above may help you realize that even if you have not had much experience with teams at work, you probably have collected more teamwork experience than you imagined. When it is time to write your essays, you should be able to tease out the necessary leadership and teamwork examples from other life situations.

One of the hallmarks of teamwork and leadership is effective and active listening. Think of examples where you took the time to listen to others patiently and skillfully and how doing so eased tensions and increased collaboration. Have you ever helped generate enthusiasm for a project when enthusiasm was flagging? Brainstormed an idea to strengthen a group or project? Helped a group in conflict to find a middle ground? These are all demonstrations of teamwork. If you've ever organized an impromptu lunch, brought in coffee and pastries to the office because everyone suffered a rough day before, lent a friendly, objective ear when others wanted to talk, offered to shoulder part of a colleague's workload when she was under unusual stress, you will demonstrate that you are a proactive and sensitive team player, a candidate for true leadership. Frankly, any time you took the initiative to get involved with other people (especially when they were difficult!) to enhance or improve a situation or create a more positive atmosphere builds the case that your MBA program of choice ought to admit you.

Organizational ability

When you are in b-school, you will not only have to juggle a rigorous course of studies but also be expected to competently handle your responsibilities in group projects, search for internships and jobs, participate in some club activities, and perhaps even maintain some semblance of family life. That's a tall order, and requires time management and other organizational skills. Naturally, if your job demanded organizational prowess, you'll want to find a way to establish that when writing about significant challenges or achievements at work. If your job only demanded average organizational skills, you'll need to establish your ability to juggle many responsibilities in other ways and show that you are not in the habit dropping the many balls you are juggling.

Organizational skills also suggest that you know how to evaluate available resources – whether manpower, money, or equipment --and use them effectively to achieve specific goals. If you haven't had the opportunity on the job, have you done so in a community service activity, such as a holiday fair, a political campaign, a charity fundraiser, or a trek? Use those experiences to show that you know how to get things done.

Communication

Working effectively in teams and being an effective leader naturally requires good communication skills. As you present yourself as irresistibly as you can as a candidate for b-school, you'll need to highlight how your skillful communication has added value to the organizations where you have worked or in which you have otherwise participated. The examples you cite in your essays should also portray your interpersonal talents. Further in the application process, you will need to be prepared to communicate effectively during interviews, a topic I'll cover fully in Chapter 8. However, as I mentioned earlier, if English is not your first language and your English abilities are less than fluent, you should invest in appropriate writing or language courses.

Why admit you?

In this chapter I have focused on the "hard" and "soft" credentials (numbers and personality strengths) you bring to your application. But the tie-breaking ingredients that may spell acceptance versus rejection or waitlist often revolve around less tangible aspects of fit as well as the distinctive and unique talents, traits and experiences you bring to the party. What is it about you that will set you apart and show that you will enhance the class? In an online chat I hosted with Liz Riley Hargrove, Associate Dean for Admissions at Duke's Fuqua School of Business[6], Hargrove explained what she looks for in the admissions process and how applicants to her school could boost their chances for acceptance: "The decision process is a holistic evaluation of an applicant's candidacy," she observed. "It's more than just your GMAT score and your undergraduate record . . . Look at the profiles on our website of students who are here at Fuqua. Find out about their stories and determine if that resonates with you. Then think about what you want to do and where you want to be and what you want to accomplish with your life, and see if there's an intersect with the stories that you've seen and heard from our current students and our alumni. If that resonates with you, then Duke's a good place for you. Look at the incoming class profiles to determine where you fit in that profile."

Hargrove also noted the diversity of backgrounds that fosters a fertile learning atmosphere: "My job is to create a microcosm of the world for our students' learning experience. That means that we'll have some students who have had tremendous international experience, and we'll have students who have managed non-profits here in the United States. We'll have students who have worked in consulting and accounting and financial services in very traditional pre-MBA careers, but we'll also have some people who have done some very non-traditional things. All of those experiences make for a really rich learning environment. So really take a step back and think about what it is you've done professionally that will give you the opportunity to contribute to your classmates' learning experience."

Even if you have chosen your target schools very carefully and know you are competitive and a good match for those programs, adcoms will still be faced

---

6   From "2011 Duke Fuqua MBA Admissions Q&A with Liz Riley Hargrove" http://www.accepted.com/chat/transcripts/2011/mba01132011_duke.aspx

with many more qualified applicants than they have room for. They will look for every possible way to whittle down the field. Their next step will be to look beyond all your basic plusses and imagine what additional, distinctive strengths you will add to the class profile. In other words, they'll want to be confident that aside from being a focused and mature team player, you might also be interested in taking over leadership of the Salsa club, whose current chairperson is graduating this year, or helping to organize the annual charity 5-K race.

Diversity is more than just race and gender

This brings us to the role of diversity in b-school admissions, which remains an important factor. If you are a member of an overrepresented applicant group, the idea of diversity may understandably induce heartburn. If, however, you are a woman from Bulgaria with sterling stats and intriguing work experience at Lloyd's of London, you may be practicing your happy dance even before you submit your applications.

The good news is that diversity refers to more than gender, race and nationality. Diversity also takes into consideration geography, specialty backgrounds, professions, and personal interests. For example, in weighing two otherwise equally qualified applicants with similar professional credentials, one from Boston or Chicago and the other from Uncertain, Texas (yes, this is a real place!), my money would be on the applicant from Uncertain. Not because of the running joke his hometown might provide the class, but because admitting someone from the Southern bayou region of the United States will likely add to the geographical diversity of the class. This, in turn, will add to the diversity of insights and perspectives this applicant can bring on a number of issues, from environmental issues to life itself.

Let's say you are from a large subgroup in the applicant pool. Here are three ideas to help you bring out your distinctiveness:

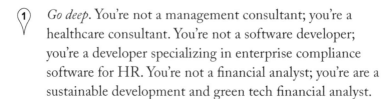

1. *Go deep.* You're not a management consultant; you're a healthcare consultant. You're not a software developer; you're a developer specializing in enterprise compliance software for HR. You're not a financial analyst; you're are a sustainable development and green tech financial analyst.

2. *Look at your nonprofessional activities.* Do you play an instrument or sing with any proficiency? Do you write poetry or belong to a gourmet cooking club? Do you have a long-standing relationship with a community group in which you have made an impact?

3. *Show how you have overcome challenges.* If you have overcome a personal hardship, disability, or other challenge, this would surely be relevant. This is not an invitation to over-dramatize the challenge or hardship or to write pity essays. Writing truthfully and without embellishment about the steps you took to overcome your challenge will be eloquent testimony to your uniqueness factor.

Looking at these aspects of diversity may strike you as utterly irrelevant to your qualifications to earn an MBA. From a purely academic standpoint, you would be right. But there's no getting around the fact that if you stand out from the crowd because you play the cello in a community symphony, spent six months in a culinary institute, developed a specialty in green tech consulting, or come from an unusual or underrepresented place, you will add interest and diversity to the class. And that is valuable to most b-schools.

I can already hear some of you groaning, "Great. Why didn't anyone tell me a few years ago I should have taken up the cello? What if I'm just too 'typical' to be noticed?" To all of you I say: Take heart. Each and every one of you is an individual, and if you have lived for twenty-five or thirty years it is almost impossible for you not to have had experiences or developed passions that will be worthy of sharing with the adcoms. Also remember that presenting yourself authentically and sincerely will add to the compelling nature of your MBA application.

The Bottom Line ←——————————————

→   **Check school websites to see if your GMAT score is competitive.** For a top ten or top fifteen program, you'll want to score in the 80th percentile on both quant and verbal.

→   **Combat a low GMAT** by following the steps outlined in the chart on Page 38.

→   **Illustrate your contributions and impact at work** and in other organizations where you have taken an active role – it's not just about the years on the job.

→   **Be prepared to display key character traits** in your essays and in interviews, including *leadership, teamwork, analytical ability, initiative, organizational ability* and *communication skills.*

→   **Show your diversity beyond race and gender** by highlighting how you have overcome particular challenges, demonstrating the unique ways you have made an impact at work or in your community, and specifying your niche beyond generic titles.

——————————————————————→

Chapter 4

Choosing the Right Schools for *You*

Find the intersection between the schools that you want and the schools likely to want you in return

So far, I've tried to illustrate why and how MBA Smarties should strategize their MBA applications before actually filling out any applications or writing any essays. Because I'm such a firm believer in the "ready, aim, fire!" philosophy of school applications (and not the reverse), the first three chapters of this book have focused on what I consider the three essential steps in this strategic process:

(1) Analyze your career goals and educational needs.

(2) Research programs you might be interested in to see which will help you achieve your goals and suit your learning style.

(3) Assess your qualifications as an MBA applicant.

All too often, applicants miss one or more of these initial steps, which can lead to a scattershot or poorly thought out approach to the applications. Without performing this due diligence, you are likely to apply to schools for the wrong reasons, such as the star quality of a school name, wanting to live near a significant other who works in that city, or having heard that the school really goes for candidates like you. But applying to schools where you don't fit is just a big waste of time, energy and money. Following a clear roadmap that is based on logic and facts, on the other hand, enhances your marketability as an applicant. It shows you know what you're about and what you are not about. It shows that you took the time to figure out where you belong. It's just smart.

Now it's time to put together the pieces of this analysis and research and get to the more exciting part of the application process: picking your schools. You can start by graphing out two big circles: One contains the names of the schools *you* want to attend. The other contains the names of the schools likely to want you in return. The schools in both circles are the ones you should apply to, or at least choose from. *The intersection of these two circles becomes the universe of schools you should consider.* Back in Chapter 2 you learned what a wealth of information is available on the websites of most well-regarded MBA programs. Now is a good time to revisit those websites to look at the class profiles and confirm that there is an overlap between your qualifications and the typical profile of admitted students at the schools that support your goals. The class profiles will show you the ranges and averages of GMAT scores, GPAs and years of work experience. Do your numbers fit in those ranges? If your quant profile is a "go," check to see if you are also a match qualitatively. After all, it's not enough to know that you can match brain cell for brain cell among your future classmates. You want to know that you'll be simpatico with the kinds of students those programs attract. How can you judge this sort of complementariness? Look at text or video profiles of students that often appear on school websites, student blogs (sometimes hosted by the schools) or on the MBA blog aggregator hella.opencoder.org. Can you imagine yourself working, studying and collaborating on projects happily with these folks?

Are you a fit or a misfit?

Let's look at a few profiles of fictional applicants and see how well they fit with the schools they have chosen:

SHANNON - *She's got excellent work experience in new media marketing and development* and a competitive GPA (3.8) and GMAT (710). Having lived her whole life in the cold Midwest, Shannon found the West Coast's sunnier climate and U.C. Berkeley's (Haas) proximity to San Francisco an irresistible lure. Given her professional chops and strong stats, she is optimistic about her chances. But a closer reading of Haas' latest curriculum enhancements revealed the school's increased emphasis on what it calls "Leading Through Innovation" and a culture emphasizing four core principles: 1) question the status quo; 2) confidence without attitude; 3) students always; and 4) beyond yourself. Despite her strengths, Shannon has no community service and limited leadership experience, making it a tough sell to show she belonged in a program so heavily geared toward the idea of leadership and "beyond yourself." *Misfit.*

CHARLIE - Since his college graduation, *Charlie has worked in real estate development and wants an MBA to move up in his real estate development firm.* His girlfriend is a student at London Business School, and Charlie is thinking about INSEAD because it is only a one-year program. Trouble is, INSEAD has few relevant courses in real estate development. As with Shannon, Charlie's other strengths in work experience and good stats cannot compensate for a mismatch of his career goals and school strengths. *Misfit.*

STEPHANIE - *An aspiring management consultant* with decent entry-level experience in a small management consulting firm, Stephanie plans to apply to Tuck, Ross, HBS, Kellogg and Darden. But her 650 GMAT puts her at a serious disadvantage. All those schools, as well as most management consulting firms recruiting from them, will be looking for GMATs of 700 or higher. *Misfit.*

DANNY - *A career changer moving from IT to financial consulting,* Danny prepared for the change by taking more quant and finance classes at a local college and volunteering as a financial counselor at a community service agency. With his 720 GMAT and 3.7 GPA, he applied to five programs, including Wharton and MIT Sloan. Denied acceptance by all schools, he reapplied to MIT Sloan the following year, showing additional growth in his financial consulting experience. *Fit.*

JUAN - With four years of media post-production experience, Juan *wanted to move up in the world of internet media production.* His 680 GMAT placed him a bit under the GMAT average at Columbia. But Juan's combination of high GPA (3.8 at UCLA), underrepresented minority status, and well-documented initiative and management abilities was a perfect for the school's media concentration. *Fit.*

CHANDRA - *Eager to move up in the world of nonprofit management,* Chandra's nontraditional background in social work made her a tough sell for MBA programs the first time she applied. This was despite her 720 GMAT, 3.9 GPA and demonstrated record of community service and leadership. Dinged by all five top-twenty programs when she applied after only two years of full-time work experience, Chandra reapplied the following year to two of the schools and expanded her reach to three others, including Duke (Fuqua), which offers a concentration in social entrepreneurship. With another year of proven commitment to nonprofit management and innovative leadership on the job, she was just right for Duke, which even offered her a scholarship. *Fit.*

How many applications are too many?

Let's say that everything is checking out in this final step in choosing your schools. What if you *still* end up with a list of ten schools that land in the happy intersection of schools you like and which may want you? Unless you have a masochistic streak (and lots of time on your hands), you will *not* want to apply to ten schools. The application process will be inordinately time-consuming, costly and draining, and you'll end up with a serious case of application burnout at the end. Who needs it? Narrow your list down to five to eight schools. That still adds up to a *lot* of essays to write and letters of recommendation to gather. Even though you will be able to recycle much of your essay material, each school's questions differ in wording and length. Many questions will be completely unique. Even questions that at first glance seem very similar are sure to contain subtle differences upon closer reading, and you must pay attention to those subtleties. Cut-and-paste jobs are also obvious to the adcoms. You will need to give each application the attention and time it deserves.

Are even five, six or seven applications too many? The question of how many applications are right is always hotly debated on numerous forums and boards, and naturally there is no single right answer. It depends on many factors, including your qualifications, the schools you are aiming for, whether you are willing to tolerate the possibility of reapplications if rejected, your goals, and whom you ask. Some advisors recommend applying to no more than three to four schools, period. I am a little less doctrinaire, but offer the following guidelines:

☑ If you have two or three schools that support your goals with acceptance rates north of 30 percent and where you are strongly competitive, then three schools should be sufficient.

☑ If you can find *only* two or three schools that support your goals and meet your needs, which happens rarely, then stick with those two or three choices.

☑ If your dream schools are intensely competitive (acceptance rates under 15 percent) and/or your qualifications are not competitive, then you should consider applying to one or two of those top-choice programs, and three to six where you will be more of a contender.

☑ If you are applying to schools with acceptance rates in the 15 to 30 percent range and you are competitive but certainly not a slam dunk (most people aren't), I suggest applying to three to six schools in this range and one or two in the range where you are likely to be accepted.

Your goals and qualifications relative to your competition are paramount. If you are from an overrepresented applicant pool, such as Indian IT males, you may want to apply at the higher end of the ranges I provided above. Don't pressure yourself needlessly by applying to all schools during the first round. If you are tackling more than three schools, your ability to produce outstanding applications within such a short time frame will be greatly compromised. Split those applications between the first two rounds, with your top choices getting Round 1 attention.

What about a stretch school? If there is a school you simply are dying to attend where you are not obviously competitive, go ahead and apply. Who knows? As the saying goes, "You'll always miss one hundred percent of the shots you don't take." But don't apply exclusively to schools that are unlikely to accept you!

When you should consider lowering the bar

What if your research reveals a gloomier picture, namely, that none of the schools you want to attend are likely to accept you? In that case, you have two options. The first: Wait a year and work to bolster your experience and credentials. Make yourself more competitive by taking more initiative on the job and signing up for quant classes. If you are really serious about becoming qualified MBA material, prove it.

The second option is to lower the bar and find other schools where you will be viewed as competitive, but which still support your career goals. When I speak to applicants who are disappointed that they are not Stanford material, I often ask them, "What is ultimately more important to you? Obtaining an MBA as a means to advance your career or having bragging rights that you went to Stanford?" In most cases, applicants would rather have a degree from a lesser known program than no MBA at all.

Finally, if even middle-tier MBA programs seem out of reach, consider alternate paths to achieve your goals. For example, you might continue to work in your field and take quant courses on the side until you qualify for an Executive MBA program, mostly geared for people who have ten years or more of work experience. Part-time MBA programs are also generally easier to get into but will still require making a case for why the MBA is important for your particular career path. In addition, many part-time and EMBA programs will want to know that you can handle the demands of full-time work and a part-time MBA program.

How about the idea of having a "safety" school? First let's clarify what a safety school is and isn't. A safe school is *not* a school that you would not attend. It makes no sense whatsoever to apply to programs that don't appeal to you. There is simply too much invested in the process. A safety school *is* one where you are highly competitive and that is strong in your area of interest but not as highly regarded overall. Despite all my caveats about relying on rankings, when it comes to safety schools, I do rely on them as a proxy for reputation. The school must still support your particular goals, but it doesn't carry the overall brand value of some of the more competitive schools.

How do you determine if it supports your goals? First, *separate professional goals from educational means:*

☑   Professional goals are what you want to do after your degree. Are graduates hired in good numbers for the positions you would like to obtain? Do the companies you would like to work for recruit on campus? Is the alumni network strong in your field?

☑   From an educational standpoint, does the curriculum teach what you want to learn, in the manner you want to learn it?

☑ Will it teach what you need to learn to pursue your chosen professional path? Are professors prominent in your area of interest?

If you conclude that no school meets the above criteria, forge ahead in your career without the additional degree. As you work hard and take initiative on the job and in improving your quant skills, you may well qualify for some sort of MBA program a bit down the line, whether a full-time program, a part-time, or executive program.

On the other hand, most of you will find programs where you are truly competitive and that still support your goals. Those programs will be your insurance policy if you are applying with a less-than-perfect profile to programs with cutthroat competition. They may also prove to be more generous with financial aid.

Applications – one at a time, please

You can do yourself a big favor by approaching the applications one at a time. To do this effectively, take out a calendar and mark the Round 1 and Round 2 deadlines for all the schools you are aiming for. (I'll talk about Round 3, which is a curious animal, a bit later.) The organizational skills that you intend to demonstrate through your essays will surely be tested during the fall and early winter months if you are applying to more than four schools, and you will need to plan carefully. Do your best to avoid working on more than three or four applications in a single round. If you are also holding down a full-time job, which the vast majority of MBA applicants are, it's hard to see how the quality of your applications will not suffer, to say nothing of your social life and sleep.

You might wonder, What difference does it make if I work on two applications at once, especially when the schools I am applying to are asking similar questions? I'm glad you asked. Each of your applications will benefit from your dedicated focus on that school. Thinking about each school's values and personality will help guide you in selecting the most relevant experiences, stories and anecdotes to write in that school's essays. To the extent that you will have choices about which experiences and stories to write about, consider which will best highlight your fit with different schools. For example, if you are applying to a school that highly values community service, you would want to discuss community service in one essay, whether the essay relates to a question on leadership, career goals or achievements. While each application should reflect you, each application will also differ in response to the specific questions and values of the school. Your reasons for choosing School A will also differ, at least to some extent, from your reasons for choosing School B.

The great Round 1 vs. Round 2 debate

"On my right, now entering the ring is Round 1. A perennial favorite with those who boast stratospheric GMATs, patents, Noble Prizes, an ascent of Everest, and highly caffeinated systems. And waving to the crowd from my left is Round 2, favored by those with more average, but still respectable scores, grades and experience."

So goes the fight over when to submit an application. I am not impressed by attempts to win the admissions game through timing, at least using these arguments, which are specious and give too much credence to minor or nonexistent factors as opposed to those that really count.

What counts above all else is the *quality* of your application. Submit your applications only when they are at their best, no matter what round. The argument that Round 1 is for superstars simply isn't true. Many superstars apply Round 2 and even later. Some applicants are absolutely determined to submit Round 1 because they want the "early advantage" and will foolishly rush their applications, putting forward lackluster presentations of themselves in a mad dash to a R1 finish line. Still, there is no denying that when you wait to apply Round 2, many seats have already been given to Round 1 applicants.

Let's call this match a draw. The boxers can take off their gloves and pull up a chair. My rule: *Apply as early as possible, provided you don't compromise the quality of your application.*

Here's a perfect example of how the theory that Round 1 is advantageous no matter your profile is just plain wrong: Over the years I have received many anxious emails from applicants who have been struggling with their GMAT scores. They want to attend a top fifteen program but are unlikely to be admitted with their current scores. These applicants are eager to apply Round 1, yet they are better off raising their GMATs and postponing applications to Round 2.

True, Round 1 tends to be a smaller pool, but it is also more clear cut. Exceptionally qualified candidates are often hellbent on getting their applications in by Round 1, while more average or typical candidates, such as those mentioned above, will also rush their applications in, believing Round 1 will give them an advantage over Round 2. Schools anticipate a bottleneck in Round 2, which may yield anywhere from two to six times as many applications as Round 1. But this fact only highlights that Round 2 is actually *more* intensely competitive than Round 1, and it is a big mistake to wait for Round 2 because you assume competition is somehow weaker in that round. Don't stress over the timing of your applications. Instead, focus on improving your profile, learning about the schools and differentiating yourself from your competition.

Is there an advantage to applying early in a round, especially Round 1? I don't think so. You are much better off holding onto a completed first application and submitting it closer to the deadline. In fact, as you work on subsequent applications, you will improve your essays and be able to relate experiences and goals with greater clarity. If you just put that first completed application away while you work on applications two and three, then you can go back and revisit the first application before that school's Round1 deadline and refine it before you submit. That first application will have benefited from your recent writing experience and greater clarity.

This doesn't mean you should wait until the 11th hour to upload your application. Servers are often overloaded on deadline day. You want to pad your deadline to take into consideration unforeseen circumstances, such as getting sick three days before the deadline or some other minor emergency that will prevent you from working on that last revision and polish of your essays. You will feel more confident in the package you submit when you have given it that final review and submitted a few days before the deadline.

Round 3: Viable option or lonely stepchild of the MBA admissions process?

MBA programs do not offer a Round 3 deadline solely to reject all comers. While a majority of the spaces available will have been offered to qualified applicants in Rounds 1 and 2, adcoms often discover stellar and highly competitive candidates in this round who add diversity to a class. Yet third-round applicants also need to realize that there are far fewer slots left by this point. An equally harsh reality is that by Round 3, grants and scholarships are harder, if not impossible, to obtain.

Those are serious downsides of a late round application. Now let's also consider the upside:

- ☑ You still have a chance of matriculating in the following fall instead of waiting an entire year.

- ☑ A few programs still give feedback to rejected applicants. That feedback could improve your applications next fall. Don't apply only to obtain feedback, but getting feedback could make applying educational and worthwhile, even if unsuccessful.

Round 3 applications make sense for you in the following circumstances:

- ☑ You applied R1, were rejected at all schools, believe you simply aimed too high and now want to apply to less competitive programs where you are likely to be admitted.

- ☑ You're ready and set; you need to go!

- ☑ You are a qualified, nontraditional applicant or member of an underrepresented group.

- ☑ You prefer to have a slight chance of acceptance now over no chance.

On the other hand, you should seriously consider postponing your application until next fall if:

- ☑ You don't have time to edit and polish your essays to perfection. If you rushed your application, the adcom members will know and it will hurt you.

- ☑ Your GMAT score is only ho-hum and you plan to retake the exam after the deadline.

☑ You won't be able to secure strong recommendations until next year.

☑ You want to improve your qualifications and need more time to do so.

☑ Your work experience is only mediocre or average; an additional year of work experience would strengthen your application.

☑ You would find rejection devastating.

☑ You are a member of an over-represented group or a very traditional applicant.

All of these circumstances argue for you to wait till next fall, when your GMAT, work experience, and overall profile are beefier and more competitive.

The Bottom Line

→ **Complete your research** outlined in Chapters 1-3 before finalizing your list of target MBA programs.

→ **Revisit student profiles on school websites and read/ watch student blogs** to make sure you're a fit with your likely classmates, academically and personally.

→ **Separate professional goals from educational means** in determining whether a program supports your goals.

→ **Graph the intersection** of the schools you want to attend and the schools likely to want you in return.

→ **Limit school applications** to seven or eight, and divide applications among the various rounds.

→ **Focus on one application at a time** for maximum effectiveness, and **apply as early as possible** provided you are not compromising quality of your application.

Chapter 5

Writing for Acceptance

"Writing is an act of faith, not a trick of grammar."
-- E.B. White

Now that all your hard work in strategizing your MBA applications is finished, we begin a new chapter, literally and figuratively. Let's turn our attention from the research, planning and tactics involved in choosing your schools to the nuts and bolts of planning, writing, and editing your essays. Your essays are not the place to reel off your accomplishments like menu items in a restaurant--that list goes in your resume. Nor are your essays the place to loudly proclaim your professional or ethnic profile. Instead, your essays are your most valuable opportunity to transcend the impersonal status of being MBA applicant number 658 with the 680 GMAT and three years as a junior analyst/software engineer/fill-in-the-blank title to a distinct and memorable individual with a voice, a passion, something important to say and something important to add to the incoming class. The clear thinking you invested in during the research phase should help you write persuasively and authentically, giving you a strong advantage over other applicants who skipped over this vital preparation and ended up writing superficially and generically.

Make the connections that matter

Outstanding MBA application essays have several things in common. One of the most important among them is successfully making connections between your past and your present, and between your present and your future. The decision makers will also want to see you make persuasive connections between your interests and your activities, and between your passions and your commitments. For example, if you claim that you are excited about working in green tech, that claim will be much more believable if you can show that you have involved yourself in some way in the field. If you haven't actually worked in green tech, what other actions have you taken to prove your interest? Have you become involved in an organization that promotes it?

Can you talk about books you have read on the subject? You can't just talk the talk. You have to walk the walk.

Conversely, an inability to connect the dots of your life creates doubts in the reader's mind: Do you really know what your goals are, either for obtaining an MBA or for your career beyond? When in doubt, the easiest step for a harried adcom member deluged with between five and ten applications for every seat in a class is to *deny*.

Soojin Kwon Koh, director of Admissions at the Ross School of Business, told me, "Essays that sparkle are ones that leave me wanting to learn more about the candidate, to get to know him or her personally. These kinds of essay are usually notable because they are genuine and allow the candidate's personality to come through. Applicants may think there is a formula or a certain story or profile to which they must conform in order to be an attractive candidate. This is just not the case. When applicants share their achievements, goals, and passions, we get a better idea of how they can both benefit from and contribute to our community. The formulaic essays–the ones where applicants have clearly tried to model theirs after someone else's–fall flat."

In this chapter I'll give you plenty of practical tools to write clearly, compellingly and with substance – no fluff or jargon cluttering the landscape. Adding these ingredients will help you make those all-important connections so that your essays will sparkle, too.

PLANNING

Before getting into the nitty-gritty of how to write terrific essays, here's a tip for those of you who are raring to go on your writing but are stymied because the schools have not released their applications yet. How can you harness that great inspiration and energy?

Think about essay topics even before the schools release their questions

MBA Smarties can make this quiet before the storm work for you, because while the exact essay questions evolve to varying extents from year to year, many question types are evergreen, such as the question about career goals. (We'll look at the career goals essay in more detail in the following chapter.)

You are also very likely to be asked how you overcame a challenge or dealt with a failure and to describe a notable achievement, if not two or three. Many schools will ask questions about your most significant personal influences, family background, and/or the values that most animate your life. *They really want to get to know you.* It's a good idea to think about these things now and start an informal journal, adding new recollections and insights as they spring to mind.

Your journal entries or notes should consist of experiences that will help you fill out the portrait of yourself that you want the admissions committee to see and that address the most common question types, such as:

- ☑ Events that had a powerful influence on you

- ☑ Notable achievements

- ☑ Activities that demonstrate your leadership, communications skills, and strength of character.

For each topic, jot down:

- ☑ The experience itself

- ☑ What you did

- ☑ Result

- ☑ Lessons learned

- ☑ Traits you revealed

Evaluating essay questions – what does the school want me to say?

When faced with a set of three or four essay questions per school, you have two challenges right off the top. First, you need to know how to evaluate the questions and figure out what the school is really looking for. Second, you need to learn how to choose the strongest and most illustrative examples and topics for each question *in a way that avoids duplication and presents you as the whole, versatile and multifaceted individual you are.* In my experience, many applicants have trouble with this, so let's start by unpacking Harvard's essay questions for the Class of 2014. This is as good a model as any to show how you can appraise your own sets of questions and answer them with maximum impact. As an aside, two of these questions are new at this writing, and applicants no longer have a choice among questions to answer. This change is not really surprising, because schools are constantly reevaluating and often updating their questions in order to elicit the fullest picture possible of their applicants. The lesson? Don't spend time writing answers to essay questions from the previous application season. You never know how much may change from one year to the next.

Harvard's 2011-12 Essay Questions:

1. Tell us about three of your accomplishments. (600 words)

2. Tell us three setbacks you have faced. (600 words)

3. Why do you want an MBA? (400 words)

4. Answer a question you wish we'd asked. (400 words)

The first two questions do not leave you much room to tell any story in detail. The best way to tackle these questions is to think of three ministories each: three accomplishments and three setbacks. That's six ministories that will yield an average storytelling time of only 200 words each. That doesn't give much space for self-reflection about these experiences, and all schools value self-reflection, so these questions will demand the tightest writing possible--no wasted words!

Question 3 allows you more elbow room for your narrative and is the perfect place to show HBS why you deserve a seat in their class. Without repeating material you used in the first two questions, maximize your impact in this essay by referring to the values the school looks for among their students. In the case of HBS, these traits (leadership, capacity for intellectual growth, and engaged community leadership) are listed right on their website under admissions criteria. Obviously, you must also somehow demonstrate an understanding of and compatibility with their famous case study method. Can you show why you are well suited to this method of study and how the kind of thinking it develops will help you in your career? The last question gives you almost total freedom, and many applicants are uncomfortable with such a blank canvas. I often have clients who will worry, What do they want me to say? Is this a trick question? What if I talk about something they're not interested in? What if I blow an opportunity to talk about something that would have really 'wowed' them?

Open-ended questions like this are a way for the school to see what else you choose to reveal about yourself, a side of you that you have not had a chance to express in the other essays. When trying to figure out what to write about here, ask yourself two questions:

- ☑ What do I want the school to know about me that they do not know yet?

- ☑ How else can I complete the picture I want the school to have of me?

Will your essays reflect work-life balance and each school's values?

As you consider all the experiences and goals you might write about, keep two words in mind: *balance* and *values*. Don't write exclusively about career-based experiences, whether accomplishments or setbacks. Write about community involvement, hobbies, playing competitive water polo, performing with a band or in a dance troupe, or the time you trekked alone through six countries in Asia. Toss some personal experiences into the mix. As a guideline, I recommend using a 2:1 ratio of professional to personal experiences, but you will always have to use your own good judgment as to the sources of your strongest material.

As you develop your list of potential topics, also ask yourself these questions:

- ☑ Do these experiences complement one another?

- ☑ Do they show different facets of my personality, strengths and involvements?

- ☑ Do I show self-reflection, lessons learned, personal growth?

Answering these questions will also help you achieve a balance of material that will create a full-bodied profile.

Each school also promotes its own set of values through their curriculum and programs. These values reflect the school's philosophy and are stated plainly on their websites. For example, Harvard's website devotes substantial paragraphs (on the Admissions Criteria page) to each of their three key criteria in applicants, which I mentioned above: "a habit of leadership," "capacity for intellectual growth," and "engaged community citizenship." The website of the University of Texas McCombs School of Business asserts that their full-time MBA program is built on four pillars: "knowledge and understanding; responsibility and integrity, communication and collaboration, and a worldview of business and society." Notice the different emphases in just these two schools. Take care to know the stated values of the schools where you are applying. When choosing what to write about, try to include experiences that reflect and resonate with each school's values.

Writing with sensitivity about a school's values does *not* mean writing what you think the adcoms want to hear. Believe me, readers in the admissions office can sniff out disingenuousness from the far side of the campus. Only write what is true and real, without exaggeration.

Light your path to great essays with a STAR

"Creativity is allowing yourself to make mistakes. Art is knowing which ones to keep." -- **Scott Adams**

Let's return to our example of Harvard's set of questions. You have six mini-stories to write about (achievements and failures) and two 400-word essays (why MBA and the open-ended question). To home in on the best possible subjects for these, grab a STAR to help light your path. STAR stands for:

Situation or Task you faced

Action you took

Results those actions generated

The STAR concept is widely used to help coach applicants preparing for job interviews, and I'll return to it in Chapter 8 to help you prepare for MBA interviews as well. When you can break down these significant professional and personal experiences into such distinct parts (situation or task, action, result) the job of writing about them meaningfully should be far less intimidating. With vivid details and lively prose, your essays will shine–possibly as brightly as a star!

Think of the essays you will write as short dramatic stories. Naturally, you are in the leading role. When I say "dramatic" stories, I do not mean that you should inflate, exaggerate or embellish any of your experiences beyond the simple truth. Aside from the obvious ethical problems of that approach, you don't need any embellishment: Your stories will automatically be absorbing when you write them with your authentic, heartfelt voice, spiced with precise and colorful details. This will be true whether writing about your most significant achievements and challenges, what you have learned from failure, the experiences that have shaped you and your values in the most fundamental, lasting way, or anything else the schools throw at you.

For example, in tackling the Harvard question about achievements, remember the importance of balance and values. Don't make all three achievements professionally related; include one from outside the office. Try to show how you have demonstrated at least some of the school's values ("a habit of leadership," "capacity for intellectual growth," and "engaged community citizenship") in your essays. Notice I said "demonstrated," and not simply parroting the school's own phrasing of their values.

The essay delights are in the details

The details and color in your examples will make your stories come alive. For a career achievement, you might write about having faced down a dragon boss for whom you could never produce enough, or fast enough, or well enough. This dragon boss's fire-breathing approach to project management naturally had devastating effects on the whole department. Over a period of months, your quiet, persistent, behind-the-scenes diplomacy with higher management and consistent efforts to keep co-workers in as good humor as possible (handing out copies of Dilbert cartoons and organizing a lottery to win a season's worth of DVDs of "The Office" was inspired, if you say so yourself), ultimately led to a happy ending: Tyranny-Sore-Us Dragon Boss was sent for long-term management training far away in the Brazilian rainforests. Illustrating the steps you took to get these results, in concrete terms, will show you as someone with leadership ability and potential. It's easy to see how well the STAR template works for this example. Use it to help break down the essential components of the stories you need to tell.

Let's take another example. If you are addressing a "failure" question prompt, you might write about the time when you were assigned an important task, yet you made a significant error in judgment or in the execution of that task. That error led to a missed deadline, a disappointment for your team, or some other black mark on your record. How did you rebound from that failure? Did you decide to pack it all in, live off the land in remote Montana, and become a recluse? Or did you look yourself in the mirror, own up to your mistake, and vow to learn from that mistake and incorporate a better way of doing things in the future? What lessons did you learn, and how have you incorporated changes since then?

WRITING

If you already have read sample essays of successful MBA applicants, you may have asked yourself afterward, "Sure, these are great, but what do these essays have to do with me? How am I supposed to write like this?"

Identifying the ingredients of a winning essay

You need to start your writing process with self-knowledge. No Google searches required! Instead, search your own internal hard drive for your experiences and your dreams. Examine your head and your heart–the source of all good material in personal essays. Then use anecdotes, specifics, and examples to reveal what's in your heart. Show that your dreams are grounded in experience.

Choose a specific theme for each essay

You first heard this advice back in middle school: Every essay needs a theme. Guess what? It's still true. Not only that, but you should be able to articulate your theme, your main point, in one sentence. Writers trying to sell a book or screenplay are expected to be able to summarize the main point of their entire book or screenplay in a ten-second sound bite. You should be able to do the same for each of your essays. Here are a few examples:

"My experience in and passion for middle-school curriculum development leads me to pursue an MBA now so I can grow in the field of educational management."

"As the child of refugees from a war-torn country, the values and influences of my family have taught me resilience, faith, and a commitment to a career in the field of government diplomacy."

"As a team lead, my failure to ensure our team met its deadline on an important product launch led me to assess my over-reliance on my own opinions and has since led to a more mature and inclusive management style."

"My first exposure to Dixieland Jazz during Mardi Gras in New Orleans when I was a kid grew into a lifelong passion for playing the saxophone, a hobby I love even more than snow shoeing."

You need to clarify your thoughts and the direction of your essay before you can summarize your theme this way. This is excellent preparation to write the essay, since the clear thinking you will have attained regarding your theme will lead to clearer, more focused essay writing. It will also help you visualize the elements your story needs to be memorable and have impact.

Answer the question – or questions

This sounds so obvious, doesn't it? But you might be shocked to learn how many people with high GPAs and stellar GMATs actually fail to answer the questions that are asked by the adcoms. If a question asks you to discuss a failure, you must come clean and discuss a time when you blew it. Implied in this question is: What have you learned from that failure? Ideally, you also will make some room to mention a time when you successfully handled a similar, subsequent situation, proving that you grew from that earlier failure.

Sometimes an essay prompt includes two or even three questions, but applicants are so focused on the primary question that they pay scant attention to the subquestions. For example, UNC Kenan-Flagler asked this on its 2011 application: *Please describe your short- and long-term goals post-MBA. Explain how: your professional experience has shaped these goals; why this career option appeals to you; and how you arrived at the decision that now is the time and the MBA is the appropriate degree.*

It's unlikely that anyone would miss the first part of the question, to describe short- and long-term goals post-MBA. But read carefully: The school is also asking three other, distinct things: 1) How your professional experience has shaped these goals; 2) Why this career option appeals to you; and 3) How you arrived at the decision that now is the time and the MBA is the appropriate degree. It will take skill to answer all four questions in only 500 words, and that tight word limit underscores the importance of mapping your content. If you focus exclusively on what you feel is the main part of a question, you may omit answering other parts of the question.

In almost any career goals or "why an MBA" question, you must also address the issue of fit with the school. Don't respond with an answer that could apply to all programs in your field. That is a nonanswer, nonstarter, and probable ding. Don't just *claim* that you are more qualified than anyone else to attend their program. Write *specifics* about that program relating to your interests and goals. Mention internship opportunities, professors doing research in your field, and other aspects of the program that have drawn you to this school to prove your interest is sincere and grounded in your career aspirations.

Structure your essay

Think of your essay as a house that you are building. You are the architect. Like a house, your essay needs a foundation, from which you must build up. In this case, your support beams are the supporting material that will furnish your essay with form and substance. Every sentence you add should build on the sentence that preceded it by offering new information and specific details that give body and context to your story. You also want to avoid repetition. Remember, avoid repetition, because it quickly becomes boring. (See what I mean?)

As you revise your drafts, you are likely to move material around or replace some anecdotes with others. That's part of the creative process, and you should welcome it. Still, it's helpful to plan your essay structure as best you can, notwithstanding eventual changes you will make later. Write an outline, even if it is general or just a rough sketch. Many people like to use a process called "organic outlining," which involves jotting down main points in just a word or two on index cards or Post-It notes. You can map your essay structure by laying your notes or cards on the table, so to speak. As you begin to visualize how the essay will grow from its essence and theme, you can physically move your key points and ideas around until you hit upon the structure that works best for the story you want to tell. Use whatever system you like best, but have some roadmap in mind for each essay.

In all likelihood, you will have to write several essays with overlapping subject matter for your different applications. And the essays lengths for essays that cover similar ground will also vary widely, perhaps from as few as 250 words to up to 1,000 words. Ironically it's much harder to write a very short, very good essay than it is to write a very good, longer one. Writing the bite-sized essay is like being six feet tall and stuck in a coach airline seat – you're going to feel cramped even when writing as economically as possible. Whether planning for the most compact essay or a comfortable 750-1,000-word essay, estimate how much space you will have for an introduction, main body and conclusion. These elements won't be equal in length, but dividing your essay into parts like this will help you gauge roughly how much you can afford to write in each section. I encourage my clients to write up to 20 percent above their essay's word limit in their early drafts since I know I will be able to trim the fat, leaving more space for the meat and potatoes (or the gluten steaks, if you are vegan) of their story. You can follow this rule as well, assuming you have an editor at the ready to help you streamline.

Grab your reader's attention – and don't let go!

It is the job of the adcom staff to read your essays. It is also their job to read many hundreds of other essays during the course of an extremely busy application season. Unless you distinguish yourself through writing that has a distinctive voice and is crisp, informative, articulate, jargon-free and authentic, you may commit the cardinal sin of boring your readers. While adcom members are professionals who take their jobs seriously, they are only human.

If need be, they will slog through every last word in every essay you submit, even if you are boring them to tears. But how much better for them – and for you!—if you keep their attention riveted by your narrative.

Good journalism features start with a captivating lead. So should your essays. A good way to think of an engaging lead is to imagine the story you are telling as a dramatic production. What would make a good first scene? What action is taking place? What is at stake? How can you make the readers care about you and what you are telling them?

You don't need to tell your story in chronological order. You can launch your scene in the past, the present, or even the future, and then weave in the necessary background information. There are endless opportunities for creative openings. Let's look at some examples:

> "As the CEO of Mega-Millions Natural Cosmetics, Inc., I am fielding questions from the podium at our annual shareholders' meeting. I feel a heady adrenalin rush as I confidently explain our plan for continued expansion into the South American market. This is the career dream that I hope to realize in the next 15 years, after earning my MBA and continuing to grow as a financial analyst in the health and beauty sector."
>
> "'You're crazy.' That's what my wife and colleagues said when I told them I planned to quit my job as a mortgage banker to pursue my passion: starting a gourmet food business. Though I had excelled quickly in my firm and had ranked among the top-ten producers for three years straight, real estate lending began to freeze during the economic crisis of late 2008. I didn't know how long I could afford to wait for the market to rebound."
>
> "Everyone was Korean in Seoul. No one was Korean in Prichard. Motorcycles and mopeds crammed Seoul's roads. Trees and flowers lined Prichard's streets. In cosmopolitan Seoul, I was a favorite son showered with attention from a large circle of extended family. In suburban Prichard,

> knowing no one but my parents, I was the only Asian child in the neighborhood."
>
> "When my boss informed me that I was expected to train, mentor and manage a new and promising analyst, I was stunned when she arrived at work that first day wearing a pink bow in her hair and glamorous high heels. I thought, Oh brother."
>
> "Could I make a persuasive sales pitch to 100 people for the business software I had just developed, though I had never done any public speaking before? When my boss asked me this question, I said, 'Of course! I'd be delighted.' But inside, I was terrified."
>
> "A recent survey by the American Animal Hospital Association revealed that 50 percent of pet owners threw birthday parties for their pets and that 68 percent dress them up during the holidays. As a pet lover myself, these statistics confirm that my fledgling company, 'Haute Doggy Duds,' has tremendous 'pet'-ential."

Each of these openings includes elements that might win the reader's attention. They offer personality, emotion, vision, surprising statistics, or a question that the reader will want answered. Your essays don't need to qualify for Pulitzer Prizes, but they do need to capture interest right out the gate and hold on to it. That way, readers will keep reading not because they *have* to, but because they *want* to. You can tie up your essay very neatly at the end by reintroducing some reference from the beginning to show where you have led your reader. This adds symmetry and a nice professional touch.

Often, applicants get stuck in writing their essays because they're still hung up on perfecting their introduction. Don't let this happen to you! Get a basic, placeholder intro down and move on. Don't spin your wheels, just move on to the body of your narrative. Don't be surprised if you enjoy a moment of inspiration for the perfect opening to your essay when you least expect it, such as in the middle of a boring department meeting!

Add insights and analysis

In MBA application essays, the "why" is usually more important than the "what." This brings us back to the importance of making connections. Great essays are not simply a list of interconnected anecdotes and experiences, even if each of them individually may have some interest. Whether writing about career goals, achievements, personal influences or even your love of Salsa dancing, it is not enough to write solely about *what* happened. Give events and decisions context by evaluating *why* things happened the way they did, explaining what factors led to the decisions you made, and providing lessons learned. Adding even a sentence or two of analysis and reflection about events in your life will demonstrate maturity, intellect, emotional intelligence, and self-awareness – all valued qualities in MBA applicants. Without insight and analysis, your essays will appear superficial.

Be yourself, distinctly

> **"***I always wanted to be somebody, but now I realize I should have been more specific.* **"** -- **Lily Tomlin**

When I ask admissions people what is the most common mistake applicants make, they usually complain that applicants write what they *think* adcom members want to hear, as opposed to what applicants want them to know. At the same time, some grad school consultants have been known to advise applicants to "do something extraordinary" to set themselves apart from the competition.

I plead guilty to encouraging all of my clients to write about what is most important to them and distinctive about them. Fortunately, there is no conflict between the two, even if you aren't from an exotic country such as Montenegro, Mongolia or Mozambique. And let's say you *are* from a more typical country of origin for MBA applicants. You can still distinguish yourself by using more precise definitions of who you are. For example, instead of referring to yourself as a South Asian engineer (and there are thousands of engineers in South Asia who apply to MBA programs), you could define yourself as an environmental engineer in Singapore who grew up in Gujarat.

The point is that you don't have to be a mutant-zombie Antarctic explorer, a conqueror of Mt. Everest, the holder of a dozen patents, or the winner of ironman triathlons to be distinctly yourself. Even though your career goals may be similar to the goals of others, no one else has lived your life, performed your exact job, and had the experiences that enable you to tell the stories that only you can tell. Choosing the events and words that are distinct to you will help the adcom know you as a one-of-a-kind personality.

Add color to your writing

"Show, don't tell," remains a cardinal rule in writing, yet one of the most common pitfalls I see in MBA essays is bland and generic writing that uses a lot of words to say very little. This sort of writing tends to assume the reader knows more than he or she does. *You* obviously know the back story and the details of your goals and experiences, but your readers don't unless you provide the necessary illustrations. Write with specifics, color and context to paint a scene for the reader. Avoid technical and industry-specific lingo that only others in your field will understand.

Here's a typical example of the kind of vague, plain-wrap and utterly forgettable sentence in a career goals essay: *"Although I have been responsible for a lot of exciting projects, I want to move into management, which may not happen on my current path."*

As a reader, I would wonder: What kind of projects? What made them exciting? Why wouldn't a management path be open to the writer? See how adding appropriate details (in bold) brings the sentence from bland to bright: *"My role as **a product manager** for **a mid-sized giftware business** has allowed me to develop my **creativity as well as communication and market research skills**. As exciting as it has been to have participated in the **planning and release of our innovative kitchen giftware with designs based on famous Impressionist paintings**, I want to move more into management, which seems unlikely at this **family-owned and managed company**."*

EDITING

Outstanding essays do not spring into the world fully formed and polished on the first draft. Writing well is an intensive, iterative process, so give yourself the gift of time to let each essay (and its writer) breathe for a day or two after writing a draft before looking at it again. Typically, our clients' essays require a minimum of two revisions, and sometimes up to five, before they are polished to a fine sheen and ready to submit. You want this process to be thoughtful, not frantic. When you do return to your essays after a brief hiatus, you may be amazed at the fresh perspective you bring to them and instantly see areas where you can strengthen them with more active language, different examples, and more colorful turns of phrase.

The editing funnel

I recommend an editing process that I call the "editing funnel," thus named because you begin your evaluation from a macro, content level for each application package. Looking at the essays *as a package*, ask yourself:

- ☑ Does each essay add something new to the reader's knowledge of you?

- ☑ Does each essay shine a light on a dimension of you not revealed in the boxes, numbers, and transcripts?

- ☑ Do the essays complement each other, building a more complete picture of you as a multi-faceted individual and MBA applicant?

After you ensure that the essays as a package accomplish all of the above, go deeper into the funnel, narrowing your focus to the individual essays. Ask yourself:

- ☑ Does each essay have a clear theme and logical structure?

- ☑ Does each essay address the question, fully and thoughtfully? Have you made sure to answer questions within questions?

- ☑ Have you repeated episodes or stories in more than one essay? If so, revise to eliminate duplication of detail.

- ☑ Have you included enough details and personal insights so that you are the only applicant who could have written this set of essays?

☑   Have you balanced description and analysis?

Finally, keep in mind the picture you want to paint of yourself to the admissions committee. Do your essays reveal the qualities and strengths that you want the adcom to see in you? Do you sound focused, thoughtful and energetic? Make sure that the voice you create on the page resonates positively.

Take a pass on passive voice

Once you are satisfied with the content of your essays, go the next level to edit for clarity, style, word usage, punctuation and grammar. This is the nitty-gritty of the editing process where you can enliven and tighten your writing. Start by rooting out passive voice as often as you can. This helps you lose the flab in your essays and pick up the narrative pace. Look at the passive construction in this sentence:

"Negotiations over the extent of the website redesign were carried out by a team of managers and myself, representing the technical team."

This 23-word sentence is informational, but it slogs along because of the passive construction. By simply moving the "doer" of the action to the head of the sentence, the author sheds five needless words and sounds much more like a leader:

"I represented the technical team in negotiations with management over the extent of the website redesign."

Here are a few other examples of passive voice, before and after they became toned and fit during the editing process. In addition to making your writing snappier and more interesting, you will save precious space, always at a premium in the tight constraints of MBA essays.

> **Flabby:** *Experience in this sector of healthcare marketing has been complemented by my experience as an advisor to an NGO in Sub-Saharan Africa* (23 words)
> **Lean:** *My healthcare marketing experience complements my experience advising an NGO in Sub-Saharan Africa* (14 words)

Flabby: *After arguments were made by our team lead about necessary changes that were needed to the product upgrade, it was determined to push back the product launch date.* (28 words)

Lean: *After our team lead argued for necessary changes in our upgrade, management pushed back the product launch date.* (18 words)

To be... or not to be?

When I worked in corporate communications, my boss refused to let me use any form of the verb "to be" in the company magazines I wrote and edited. His inflexibility drove me crazy, because sometimes things simply *are* and no good substitutions exist. I would never hold a client to the same standard, but you may be surprised at how often you can find a more active way of writing than using "is," "are," "was" and other forms of the verb "to be."

Flabby: *She is a skillful negotiator.* (5 words)
Lean: *She negotiates skillfully.* (3 words)

Flabby: *I was the one who made the decision.* (8 words)
Lean: *I decided.* (2 words)

Flabby: *She was able to fix …* (5 words)
Lean: *She fixed…* (2 words)

Ditch the clichés

I once read an interview with a recent grad which read in part:

> *"As a new company in a new space, we need to exceed client expectations, so first and foremost I drive client projects in the health-care and telecom verticals. But my job requires an internal focus as well, and I spend a ton of time both building and updating scalable systems, from knowledge management to invoicing and payroll."*

Huh? What "new space" was he talking about? Outer space? And what does "drive client projects" mean? Drive the clients crazy? Drive them to lunch in a new Prius? This fellow may be highly intelligent but we can't appreciate his smarts when he has fallen into the trap of meaningless business jargon that tells us absolutely nothing.

Now let's look at the same sentence, translated from business jargon to English:

"As a new company entering a new market, we need to impress our clients with outstanding performance. I personally manage projects for clients in the health-care and telecom industries, but in addition to serving our clients, I am striving to build our business by ensuring that all our systems from personnel to invoicing support our growth."

Don't bury your story in mindless clichés. "Leveraging best practices," "infrastructure strengths," "mature quality processes," "scalable systems," "industry benchmarks," "architected summaries," "core competencies," "synergies," "paradigm shifts," "high performance culture," and "thinking outside the box" are among the many tired phrases that will actually box in your writing in a muddled mass of mindlessness.

Write simply, plainly and meaningfully. Your essays and readers will thank you for it!

How does it sound? Read it aloud!

After you have replaced passive with active voice and booted your colorless, generic writing out the door, print your essay and read it out loud. Reading your work aloud is a very different experience from reading it silently on the screen, and it is extremely useful. When you listen to the words you have written, you will catch small mistakes that your eyes glossed over after so many readings, and you will also hear phrasing that you can strengthen.

In the next chapter, we will look at how to maximize the potential of specific essays types: goals, achievement/leadership, failure or setback, family background/personal influences, and the optional essays.

The Bottom Line

→ **Make connections** between your past and your present, your present and your future, and between your passions and your commitments in your essays.

→ **Illustrate self-reflection, lessons learned and personal growth** through your essays. **Consider a school's values** when choosing experiences to write about.

→ **Apply the STAR concept in writing your essays:** Situation or Task you faced, the Action you took, and the Results those actions generated.

→ **Identify a theme for each essay** whose main point can be summarized in one sentence.

→ **Captivate your readers' interest** by writing in lively, specific prose.

→ **Avoid clichés, bland and generic writing, and passive voice.**

→ **Edit for clarity and read your work aloud** for further fine tuning.

The Blooper Essay:
"Achieving Feets I Could Not Imagine"

Maybe you were writing at 2 a.m. when you were nearly giddy with fatigue. Or perhaps you confused "waste" with "waist" or "C-section" with "sea-section." Perhaps English isn't your first language (or maybe it is!), or you had a little Freud on the brain. Any of these circumstances can lead to the unintended "blooper" line in your essay. Misspellings, misuse of words, mixed metaphors, tangled syntax, even a single, solitary missed letter in a word can all conspire to some unintended hilarity on the page. The following "essay" (using a generous term) is comprised 100 percent of actual bloopers our editors have encountered over the years. Makes you want to make sure you have an eagle-eyed editor, doesn't it?

As a sales representative for the P____ Professional software, I managed the Caribbean. I had to be creative and integrate our system in their back-end thus adding value and getting them to enter their trades, which were the desired results. I told them I would dedicate a year to see the projects in the Caribbean come to fruition, so any effort would not go to waist due to turnover and shaky leadership. I therefore established a leadership development program by defining a leadership model, conducting assessments, and organizing manager saloons. In the time I worked there I assisted on numerous asses but took part in the interviews, testing, and repost construction of the last twenty. I felt I had the internal locust of control.

The raving client commendations caught the eye of our senior management. After this incident, my Site In-charge withdrew me from control room operations and assigned me for supervision of field instruments erection. He has a knack for sticking up a chord with all that he comes in contact with. Given a second chance, I would not have tried to make my business partner as an escape goat for the overall failure. As part of the planning team, my tasks involve coordinating between the various groups, setting timelines and expectations and overlooking the project plans. I have no direct budget, only ad-havoc.

Coming in as an outsider to America was a personal growth experience. I learned how many material things around us are unnecessary, the power of servitude to others, and to value my experiences and opportunities. I thus decided to live in an apartment with three Spanish roommates. They embraced me, hanging out with me and teaching me about cultural nuisances like eating dinner at ten and going out at two in the morning. It was my first brush with poverty; one that soldered in my mind, my career aspirations for life.

In flat organization there is certain bit of anatomy and entrepreneurial spirit that makes me an independent individual contributor and independent thinker. These certificates were required from more than ten different public organs… The sense of making impact is unraveled.

I would be described as a Secure Risk Taker who responds well to situations of stress and understands that risk in a calculated amount remains beneficial to coagulate deadlines at hand. I am interested in being able to develop dynamic process of continually creating new business models, improving customer experience, and opening new markets – as well as lunching new products. Because of traveling from an early age, I was constantly exposed to different foods. I think Starbucks is a public company owned by Magician Johnson, right? There are so many choices for diners that a chef not only needs to sever meals of excellent quality and consistency, but must also constantly innovate their own menus to lure their patrons back. I was excited to try new things and wasn't squeamish about things like muscles or escargot. The icing on the cake was when my chef Dr. Yip came over to me to congratulate me for having efficiently worked with one of the most difficult costumers he had had to face at General Motors.

The seeds of my interest in math and computer science were sown during my Bachelors degree and in line with my irreprehensible desire for learning. I jumped into Math and Computer Science at the first opportunity. In order to facilitate this process, while communicating the latest feature specification I started off our discussion by specifying a few specifications and urged the team to extrapolate on the initial list of specifications and develop to the full required specification based on their experience. In one word, I emerged out of my college with a desire to excel and a drive to lead. I will maintain a maniacal focus on my research productivity. I have to appear for a certification exam and as usual doing last minute cramping.

As the world is getting increasingly flattened, I intend to not only learn from the US experience, but also from the lessons of South America or India, without which my global perspective would be incomplete. I need to develop my skills to address my long-term goal of revamping the region's privates sector. While I need to taut my achievements, I believe that the ability to motivate people, whether employees, investors, partners, or the pubic, is crucial. And I'm doing online research for finding institutions that support and provide funding for primates. I will join a global venture capital firm as an investment manager focusing on undeserved markets.

Here comes my need to have a MBA degree at this juncture. An MBA will be my jetpack to elevate me from an observer position to that of a transformer. I am anxiously looking forward to enjoy the thrill of the ___ School of Business propulsion and satisfy my urge of being the tamer of rampaging healthcare cost. Furthermore, ___ offers the best all around learning environment, where I as a student am rigorously pushed to expand my limits achieving feets I could not imagine. I've decided not to rush for Columbia as this is my dream school and given the state of my application, I think I have virtually zero chance to get in for the last round this year. I hope I've made a conscious decision.

Chapter 6

How to Handle Specific Essay Types: Goals, Achievement/Leadership, Failure, Personal Influences and Optional Essays

In this chapter I'm going to focus on how MBA Smarties can make the most out of the most common essay types. All MBA applicants will grapple with some version of the goals and achievement/leadership essay prompts, and a majority will also have to find meaningful and insightful ways to answer questions about their most significant personal influences and/or times that they failed in carrying out a mission or project. In the examples below, you will see how the writers effectively answered these questions, incorporating the tips I offered in Chapter 5: writing with precision, color and active voice, while avoiding jargon and clichés.

GOALS ESSAY

"Setting goals is the first step in turning the invisible into the visible. " -- **Tony Robbins**

Approach

I have emphasized the importance of making connections in your essays – between your past and present, between your present and your future, and between your passions and commitments. A great career goals essay weaves together all these connections with the result that *your career vision makes sense in light of your experiences and influences so far.*

Even in this age of GPS navigation, I still recommend charting this essay using a trusty **MAP**. My MAP stands for **M**otivation, **A**spiration, and **P**erspiration, and an outstanding goals essay includes all three essential ingredients:

Motivation: What inspires you? Why have you made the decisions you have made? What propels you to choose your particular field? Your particular school?

Aspiration: What is your vision? Where are you headed? What do you plan to do immediately after you've earned your MBA? What about 10 years later?

Perspiration: When have you worked hard in this field or a related one? How have you demonstrated your commitment to your to your job, your personal life, or society? How do you continue to show that dedication now?

There are different types of goals essays with different wording, and as I mentioned earlier, you cannot use a one-size-fits-all approach to MBA goals essays. Tailor your answer to the specific questions, the particular school, its personality and values. And don't forget to answer the second (and third) questions that follow the first one!

Here's a great example of two opening paragraphs in a career goals essay that asked, "Briefly assess your career progress to date. Elaborate on your future career plans and your motivation for pursuing a graduate degree at_____."

✐ *Example: The next Donald Trump (without the flamboyant hair)*

> Horns blare as tiny auto-rickshaws, juggernaut buses, and bicycle-powered school buses interweave at impossibly close range in the narrow streets of Old Delhi. Exhaust fumes turn white handkerchiefs brown. I had come to India, my homeland, in March 20-- to explore the possibility of developing environmentally sustainable real estate there. Environmentally sustainable buildings produce less air pollution while conserving water and power, both subject to outages nationwide. My long-term career goal is to work as an investment executive in this rapidly evolving real estate market, contributing to environmentally friendly development. My interviews with several international real estate developers confirmed that while the infrastructure-related challenges of modern India are intense, they also present a chance to make a difference.

My interest in real estate evolved from my travels throughout the U.S., which revealed the disparity in quality of life between compact, ideally planned communities such as Boulder, Colorado and sprawling cities such as Phoenix, Arizona. Reading *The Art of the Deal* by Donald Trump, I was fascinated by creatively structured real estate deals and the potential of quality real estate to improve lives, serve as functional works of art, and generate financial returns. Real estate seemed flush with entrepreneurial success stories; I wanted mine to be among them.

✓ What works

Notice how the writer, Marty, included all three ingredients of the MAP. He also sets the scene with vivid language – we can almost feel ourselves bumping along in one of the rickshaws. By the second sentence, we can almost feel the "perspiration" – he has traveled halfway around the world to research the feasibility of his dream. In these jargon-free, cliché-free paragraphs, Marty also attests to the need for the work he wants to do in sustainable real estate development and the growth potential for the function he wants to play as a real estate investment executive. In the second paragraph, he shows us both motivation and aspiration, explaining how his career vision evolved through very specific anecdotes and details. By the end of these paragraphs, we are convinced that he is well suited for this field based on experience, abilities, knowledge of industry trends and enthusiasm.

Convincing goals essays also focus on specific career achievements and leadership initiatives. In the next two paragraphs, observe how Marty builds on the architecture of his essay by highlighting his career growth and displaying commitment to his field through extracurricular involvements. Notice that he includes specifics: working eighty hours a week, managing a team of ten, and working on a steering committee of a nine-hundred-member group. He is also very specific in enumerating the types of projects he has done and for whom. Nothing is vague here. Each sentence adds to the knowledge of the candidate:

To study investment real estate, I joined ____ Real Estate Advisors in 20__ as an analyst and was trained in finance, market analysis, and sales. It was a high-stakes environment that often demanded 80-hour workweeks. Since then, I have performed economic, zoning/entitlement, and site-feasibility research, produced sophisticated financial models and delivered research-intensive presentations to major investment firms. Today, I manage a team of 10 in the sale of development sites and existing buildings while also prospecting for new sales and managing seller expectations in a difficult market. These interpersonal and strategic aspects of the business are by far the most challenging and crucial.

My interest in sustainable real estate also evolved from my experience with the _____ Group, a global research and education organization devoted to responsible land use and the creation of thriving communities. I now serve on the board of the 900+ member Young Member Consortium, where I influence programming, direct the group's overall vision, and connect young members with seasoned practitioners.

Short-term versus long-term goals

Many schools still ask you to discuss both your short- and long-term career goals. Although you should be able to distinguish between these in just a few sentences, if you haven't thought through the differences in detail, you can get further clarity in your own mind by asking the following questions:

☑ What industry do you envision yourself in during both stages?

☑ What type of company would you work for along the way? Can you name a company that you would ideally like to work for?

☑ What do you want to do? What would your ideal position be at each of these stages? Use specific examples of job titles and real companies you might like to work for to further illustrate how much you've thought about your future.

☑ What explicit goals or milestones would you like to achieve at each stage?

☑ What impact do you hope to have on the people you work with and in your chosen field?

Here are two examples of how short-term and long-term goals can be articulated. While both are brief, they each include enough detail to convince the reader that the applicants have given careful thought to how their career dreams might be achieved. In the second example, the writer had more room to elaborate on the distinction between short- and long-term plans:

(1) My short-term goal is to return to ___ Real Estate Advisors, moving into their International Real Estate Development arm as a senior analyst and helping the company build its portfolio of environmentally friendly residential and commercial real estate. Longer-term, I hope to work as an investment executive with an international real estate developer with expertise in sustainable development, such as Hines or ___.

(2) My short-term goals are to strengthen my position at ____ Products and to break though the "glass ceiling" that I feel I have reached. As a young female in a company where most of my superiors are men with MBAs, I am eager to earn my own degree, build on my managerial and negotiating skills, and grow in a management capacity, particularly as the company works to re-brand two product lines to appeal to a younger demographic. An MBA from Haas will help me distinguish myself in the field of health and beauty product development.

Longer term, I hope to launch my own line of health and beauty products, working alongside my father, an innovative chemist with experience in health product development. Even now, we are researching market trends, networking, and brainstorming ways to make our mark as a family business in this burgeoning field.

Why an MBA now? And why choose our school?

Many schools also ask "Why is now the right time for you to earn an MBA?" or "What do you hope to gain from the XYZ program?" under that same essay prompt. Make sure to leave enough room to write knowledgably and enthusiastically about your program. This will be easier if you have made campus visits, attended student recruitment meetings, participated in chats, read school blogs, communicated with current students or recent alumni and otherwise familiarized yourself with the program and the courses and specializations it offers. In the following example, see how Marty mentions specific majors, classes, and industry-specific clubs and related activities for his

Kellogg application. Noting his observations from having sat in on a professor's class also reminds the adcom that Marty took the trouble to visit the school:

> Kellogg will help me achieve my goals through a tailored curriculum with a strong core, career advising, and global alumni base. The Management & Strategy and Finance majors, and courses such as "GIM" and "International Business Strategy," directly address my needs. As I observed in Professor Lenzo's strategy class, Kellogg's blend of experiential teaching methods felt natural to my learning style. I was further impressed when my guide, Hugh ___, '10 mentioned that he knows nearly all of his classmates. I look forward to sharing my knowledge and real estate connections; I will learn much from my classmates. I will refine my leadership skills through applying classroom knowledge to active roles in the India Business and Real Estate Clubs, the Real Estate Conference and leading Kellogg's first Real Estate Trek to India.

And here is an example from Chuck, who makes a good case for why he chose Columbia for his EMBA:

> Columbia's educational curriculum and location in the world's financial capital will help me understand international business topics as well as how the economy functions in an increasingly global economy. As an aspiring executive in the field of finance, I will be able to immediately apply the lessons I learn on Saturday at JPMorgan Chase on Monday. Additionally, Columbia's week-long International Seminar is an exciting opportunity to discuss relevant economic issues with local business and government officials in the designated country and will bolster my knowledge of cross-cultural practices and the nuances of different business cultures.
>
> I am also drawn to the school's Program on Social Intelligence (PSI) and its innovative blend of psychology and social sciences in business. My experiences in business have made it abundantly clear that correctly perceiving the dynamics of relationships in the workplace is pivotal in order to succeed. Understanding human interactions and engaging people appropriately is essential to thrive in a client-serving role like investor relations. Through PSI, I welcome the opportunity to strengthen my understanding of relationships and further attain the soft skills that the business world demands.

As you plan and write your goals essays, see if you can achieve this same level of content-rich, precise language, with each sentence adding to your dynamic profile.

ACHIEVEMENT/LEADERSHIP ESSAYS

Essays that ask you to write about significant achievements fall under the category of what are known as *behavioral* or *experiential* questions. The basic assumption behind these questions is that past behavior is a great predictor of future behavior. They are all varieties on the theme of "Tell us about a time when you..." These questions are meant to take the measure of your managerial potential.

Approach

Achievement questions present fantastic opportunities for you to reveal the uber-value of business schools: leadership. No question about it, great managers are leaders. To the extent you can display leadership through your achievement or other behavioral-related essays, you will want to do so.

Stanford GSB's essay questions for 2012 offer candidates several opportunities to illustrate instances of leadership and achievement. They include:

> **Option A:** Tell us about a time when you built or developed a team whose performance exceeded expectations.

Like most experiential questions, this essay requires specifics to be effective. Notice that the school is not asking you to list *all* the times that you may have built or developed a team. It wants to know about "*a* time," a specific incident when your performance exceeded expectations. It wants to see how you can relate your role in this success. When thinking about how to answer this kind of question, ask yourself: When did you build a team that faced challenges and succeeded? What were the expectations? What impact did your team have and how did it exceed expectations?

> **Option B:** Tell us about a time when you made a lasting impact on your organization.

This question provides an opportunity to show a different facet of your experience and personality. If you were answering this question, you should avoid writing about leadership in general terms and focus instead on the specific aspects of your contribution and its impact. How did you garner trust, organize your group, empower them, and achieve your goal?

Here is one essay that effectively addressed the question asked in Option B:

✎ Example: The Change Agent

When I was invited to become the Vice President and General Manager at Third Way Associates (TWA) two years ago, the company was in financial and administrative disorder. Employee retention was poor, and TWA took too long to pay vendors because of poor communication and accounting processes. Cash flow was managed based on immediate needs rather than by the logic of budgets planned by project and city. Sloppy expense reports that were turned in with no receipts were reimbursed to employees.

TWA founders Scott W__ and Glenn L____ had good intentions, but spent most of their time selling sponsorships and getting new clients rather than directing and managing the company. As we begin 2011, TWA is much healthier in every way. Under my direction, vendors are paid in an average of 20 days from date of invoice, instead of 60 days or more. Our cash flow is better administered since I introduced very specific detailed area budgets with over 125 budget lines per city. Because I can give the company founders much better stability and macromanagement vision, the three of us are able to look more to the future rather than simply put out fires.

Despite the difficult economy in 2010, we not only retained our same clients but also signed several new client agreements for three years or more, including a two-year contract with Puma worth $1.3 million. I've brought fresh accounts and industries into TWA, including _____ Airlines and Gatorade, among others. Combined, these accounts generated more than $500,000 in 2010 and we estimate close to $1 million dollars in 2011.

Since my arrival, we have a much wider and broader sales menu which has been crucial to generate more revenue. I've expanded our most popular sports events to 25 cities, giving our clients new investment opportunities. These events range from recreational soccer clinic tours to professional soccer games broadcast on TV.

I also expanded our field staff, and at present we have 25 strong and reliable managers who report directly to me from each city. Despite the economy, 2010 was not a bad year for TWA, and 2011 promises to be even better if we continue our current strategy and continue to work as a team.

✓ *What works*

In every paragraph, this writer mentions concrete measures he took to introduce order to a chaotic company that was trying to grow. From instituting budgets with line items, an improved accounts payable system, and recruiting additional big-name accounts, it's clear that the organization was substantially strengthened by his efforts.

> *Option D:* Tell us about a time when you went beyond what was defined or established.

This is a very broad question and my suggestions for addressing the other two questions hold here too. You should respond to this question if it allows you to demonstrate the individuality and initiative that Stanford values, but in a setting other than those you have used earlier.

✐ *Example: Forging a New Team*

I arrived in Chicago in the summer of 20__ as tech lead to revamp the website of a large chain of hotels. My company, Bright Zone, was in an uncommon position as subcontractor to a management consultancy. I discovered that my coworkers' morale had been falling for the last four months, a casualty of negative attitudes and the widely perceived incompetency of the previous firm that had been hired for the website overhaul, which had ended in disaster. I had been hired to direct development, but that was like putting out small brush fires when the whole forest was burning. I pursued team unification.

I invited the three other members of my team, as well as the client and the two management consultancy representatives, for meals and drinks after hours, and even the occasional racquetball match. I theorized that if people enjoyed each other socially, it would be harder to vilify each other at work. Over many dinners, the other techs under my supervision as well as the consultants seemed to begin to actually like each other and began trusting my recommendations.

Two months in, I realized that most of the negativity came from Barry, one of the consultants. I saw that his combative attitude toward the client was alienating us further and further from the client accepting our recommendations. This was tricky because Barry was very senior to me and also a friend. Still, I urged him to stop arguing and insisting on his own way. When his attitude and actions did not budge, I pulled a vice-president and our chairman aside and stressed that Barry's negativity was untenable and that he needed to leave our team. This was well outside my established responsibilities. My friendship with Barry complicated this dynamic, but I believed for my team to succeed we had to purge toxicity. After two weeks of meetings and interventions he was fired.

With Barry's negativity removed, my social activities began to have a dramatic impact. We became a true team as the other consulting company now trusted us and gave us broad influence to the client. In moving beyond a tech lead's responsibilities, I helped build a multimillion-dollar, strategic account.

✓ *What works*

The last two lines at the end of the first paragraph signal to the reader that the applicant saw his role as far greater than what had originally been envisioned: "*I had been hired to direct development, but that was like putting out small brush fires when the whole forest was burning. I pursued team unification.*" From there, the writer shows how he went outside the strict parameters of the job to address the negative team dynamics. As always, the specifics are critical: inviting team members out for meals, talking privately with key players, and pushing to remove a toxic element from the team.

As you sift through your inventory of significant achievements to select the winning entrants in your essays, think about these questions to help you frame answers of substance:

1. What was the obstacle, challenge, or problem that you solved in this accomplishment—a tight client deadline? A complex merger transaction? A new product launch amidst fierce competition?

2. What did you do to rise to the challenge you are writing about—motivate your team to work overtime? Sell senior management on the deal's long-term upside? Identify a marketing profile for your product that no competitor can match?

3. What facts demonstrate that your intervention created a "happy ending"? Did your team submit the project deliverables three days early despite being 20% understaffed? Your client approved the $500 million merger, the largest ever in its industry? Your new product has 20% market share after only one year? What was the impact of your leadership?

If these questions remind you of the STAR approach discussed earlier, I'm glad you've been paying attention! The STAR structure is a great approach when responding to behavioral questions.

Another tip: When writing about achievements and leadership, look for opportunities to incorporate strong verbs that illustrate your strengths in these areas. Good examples of leadership might incorporate several of the following:

- ☑ Listening
- ☑ Initiating
- ☑ Mentoring
- ☑ Teaching
- ☑ Persuading
- ☑ Organizing
- ☑ Establishing a goal or vision
- ☑ Motivating
- ☑ Managing
- ☑ Obtaining buy-in
- ☑ Taking responsibility

FAILURE ESSAY

Legendary UCLA college basketball coach John Wooden once said, "Failure is not fatal, but failure to change might be." When schools ask you to write about a time that you failed, what you learned from a setback, or what you have learned from a mistake, you have a terrific opportunity to show qualities that MBA adcoms prize: self-reflection, self-awareness, resilience, perseverance, and commitment to professional and personal development.

Yet essay questions dealing with failure, risk, mistakes and difficult interactions cause applicants to cringe, squirm and bite their nails. After all, you want to show yourself succeeding and conquering the world in your application essays, not falling flat on your face. Schools ask these questions because they want to see how you get up, how you grow following setbacks. Do you smile and try again? Do you view the stumble as temporary? Move on? Applaud effort? Accept a helping hand when offered?

No one goes through life with only successes. Thomas Edison, the prolific inventor and businessman whose experiments led to the development of the telephone, the phonograph, and the light bulb, famously said about his many scientific endeavors, "I have not failed. I've just found 10,000 ways that won't work."

Turning failures into successes

Just as Edison reframed his setbacks as the persistence that eventually leads to success, so should you. MBA Smarties portray setbacks as growth opportunities, even occasions of achievement. Unafraid to acknowledge a "blew it" moment, they demonstrate through their actions that they know how to turn failure into success, thus revealing resilience and character.

Approach

Here are some good general rules to keep in mind when approaching the failure/setback essay:

☑   Avoid blaming others for a failed project or initiative, even if others contributed to the setback.

☑   Remember that the *why* is usually more important than the *what* in MBA essays. State the failure or setback succinctly and matter-of-factly, and devote the majority of the essay to your reflections about why it went wrong, what you learned and how you have acted differently as a result.

☑   Demonstrate the steps you have taken to avoid similar mistakes since the "Oh-no!" moment. Be specific about how you picked yourself up, improved, persisted, and ultimately succeeded.

The following essay answers the question, "Describe a failure that you have experienced. What role did you play, and what did you learn about yourself?" See how Julie owns her mistake and takes concrete steps to improve her performance.

✐ *Example: Subduing righteous indignation*

Shortly after joining the Milwaukee Women's and Children's Center as a case manager, I met with a city case worker about my client, Ms. G___. Though my client met all the requirements for shelter extension, her application was denied. My repeated calls to this case worker ended in frustration. Either the phone was busy or I was shuffled like a deck of cards among departments. When I finally met with her to discuss Ms. G___'s situation, I discovered some clerical mistakes on the record. Although this was the city agency's error, I was told that Ms. G___ still had to wait several weeks for an approval. At that moment, I lost my temper.

I told the case worker that her mistake could cost my client, a mother with three small children, a place to sleep at night, leaving her inexcusably vulnerable, especially with an abusive ex-husband possibly looking for her. I also threatened to file a complaint through the Legal Aid Society against the city agency, because my client had also been denied an interpreter, even though by law she was entitled to interpretation services.

The case manager became defensive, noting the mountain of applications on her desk. In response, I questioned her work ethic, and our conversation descended into a no-win argument. I left her office indignant and empty-handed. I had failed miserably in my role as an advocate for my client's rights, having allowed my raw instinct and inexperience to prevent me from achieving my objective, which was to seek a shelter extension approval. I should have remained calm and cooperative, but instead I instigated a fight. In hindsight, it was obvious that the case worker might have been more receptive to my claims had I shown more empathy for her position, which was as a woman with far more cases to deal with than there were city resources.

After this disaster, I vowed to be more careful about controlling my emotions. Prior to going into meetings with potential for conflict, I organized my thoughts by writing them down and reminded myself of my objectives. I also sought advice from seasoned colleagues, conducted research, or contacted peer organizations when I faced situations that were new to me or where I wasn't sure of the right path. And when situations did turn tense, I learned to hold back before I spoke, making sure that what I say would not hamper achieving my objectives. With practice and self-discipline, I have gradually improved in this area. I realized that my effectiveness as an advocate for my clients required me to be cautious and thoughtful, even in the face of bureaucratic snafus. I have since received excellent feedback from my clients and formed more constructive relationships with our associates at various government agencies, including this same city case worker.

✓ *What works*

This example works well because Julie honestly reveals a personal weakness based on youthful inexperience. She also acknowledges that the pace of change for self-correction was a slow but steady process, with provable results: excellent feedback from clients. In this way, Julie shows her personal and professional growth.

✍ *Example: Catching a costly calculation error*

In 2006, my team at ___ Realty listed Pacific View Apartments, a 400-unit, 20-acre property, for $105 million. My first responsibility was to manage a team of five to quickly construct a marketing book to the standards of our very detail-oriented client for this development, located in one of the nation's hottest investment markets.

After leading a meeting to collect the team's marketing ideas, I created a timeline to produce the book while assigning research tasks to my team, coordinating the site and aerial photography, mapping, and graphic design efforts. Pacific View's rents were below market value due to mismanagement, and I feared investors would undervalue the asset. Therefore, I devised a tool that allowed them to calculate market rents by overlaying a base rent with values for every conceivable premium, such as location on the bottom or top floor, view type, and finish level. Based on their assumptions for the values of each premium, investors could calculate the building's rent potential. I also created a unique site map in which each floor plan was color-coded to enable investors to visualize the layout.

After the launch, I received a call from Kurt, one of Pacific View's owners. Kurt thought he had found an error in my financial analysis, so together we reviewed 20 pages of calculations while I explained my methodology. Although the issue he had flagged was not an error, I offered to check the calculations. Then, I noticed an actual error—I looked on in disbelief. While no one knew this error existed, it affected the cash flows so I had to reveal it. My boss was angry at the awkward position it put us in, and I thought I would lose my job. That day, I issued corrected financials and thanked Kurt for helping to detect the error. Fortunately, our attentiveness to his requests eventually helped us regain his confidence.

This experience taught me many things. First, I'd rather live honestly with a failure than dishonestly with success. Knowing how a single missed detail can invalidate weeks of work, I have also installed numerous automated error checks in subsequent financial models. Finally, handling errors ethically and responsibly is as important as avoiding them. Admitting my error and taking quick action to correct it allowed us to rebuild trust. Fortunately, we sold Pacific View at record pricing for a pre-1990 built Northern California asset, and we exceeded Kurt's expectations.

✓ *What works*

Glenn's actions of owning his mistake, taking immediate steps to correct it, and even thanking a third-party for helping to uncover the error, all show maturity and honesty. Mentioning the new error checks he installed to avoid repetition of similar mistakes also shows commitment to improve professionally. Like Julie in the first example, Glenn also exemplifies self-awareness and a commitment to turning setbacks into opportunities.

PERSONAL INFLUENCES ESSAYS

In trying to get to know how you became the person you are today, many schools will ask variations on the question: What or whom has influenced you most? Sometimes the question asks you to discuss family background and influences; other questions ask you about what matters to you most and why.

Approach

Some clients are less than thrilled to have to discuss their personal backgrounds, especially when they are from cultures that are more private. You don't need to violate your zone of privacy in these questions, but you do need to illustrate what values move and motivate you, or how people and events have shaped you to live and think in specific ways. It's entirely natural for people to talk about family influences, but those essays can easily become hackneyed and predictable if you don't go beyond talking about your grandmother reading you bedtime stories as a child and feeling loved. Instead, show how your grandmother's commitment to your education led you to become a volunteer tutor during college or how your family's passion for breathtaking treks through Costa Rica and the Grand Canyon inspired you to want to go into the field of land management.

Here are excerpts from three essays that illustrate the variety of ways these personal influences questions can be handled, and how applicants connected their previous experiences with their future goals. As always, let the question be your guide.

The first excerpt is from an essay answering the question, "What matters most to you, and why?" While it is not necessary for a writer to connect their personal influences/values to their career, Barry was able to do so in the following example.

✐ *Example: Exploring new vistas*

> When I was 5, my family took a road trip to southern Turkey from our home in Istanbul. I remember feeling exhilarated just hearing unfamiliar

Turkish dialects, the foreign feel of the countryside, and the dawning realization that there the world was much bigger than what I knew living in a big city. This early exhilaration with travel led me to explore almost two dozen countries in the world, from Taiwan to Grenada. To this day, experiencing different cultures and developing a better understanding of the world is what I am most passionate about. . .

Two years ago, I traveled to Thailand to explore my fascination with Asian culture. I found the complicated Thai script hard to learn and understand and mostly relied on my patchy Thai to converse with the locals to get around. This immersive experience enabled me to experience firsthand the Thai hospitality and famous smile that all Thais seemed to have on their faces, despite widespread poverty. I was also amazed to see that the people in Thailand smiled not only to express happiness, but also as a way to deescalate conflicts. This was a pivotal lesson that I apply in my own life: When I find myself in a tense situation or conversation, I consciously remember to smile. In most cases, my smile helps calm the people around me and defuse tension. This learning experience in Thailand was something that no book or documentary could substitute.

My love of travel and exploring new cultures has also had exciting implications for my career. When I visited Turkey in 2009, I met Mehmet, a metal artist who created phenomenal copper jewelry with elaborate and unique designs. He dreamed of supporting his family as an artist, and while I saw that some of his works could easily sell for hundreds of dollars in the U.S., in Turkey he could only sell them for a few dollars and was vulnerable to exploitation from predatory local wholesalers. I met many other artisans like Mehmet in Thailand and Mexico who shared similar dreams in poor business environments. These artisans inspired me to create "Global Caravan," an online retailer that sells unique artistic jewelry with fair trade practices. My goal is to spread the seeds of fair and ethical trade, one partnership at the time, across the developing world, providing more artisans a chance at greater prosperity. Global Caravan became profitable in just six months and has also taught me what it takes to start a business from scratch, establish relationships, write a business plan, develop a winning marketing strategy and manage sales. . .

Mark Twain's perspective on exploring the world deeply resonates with me, especially when he wrote "Twenty years from now you will be more disappointed by the things you didn't do than by the ones you did. So throw off the bowlines, sail away from the safe harbor. Catch the trade winds in your sails. Explore. Dream. Discover."

✓ *What works*

Barry's early travels with his family sparked a lifelong love of cultural exploration, a passion he has proven by listing recent travel experiences. He also writes vividly about language, place, and even the cultural and economic circumstances of people he encounters, bringing the reader right next to him for the ride. As a bonus, Barry is able to tie his commitment to travel to a professional sideline of selling fair trade crafts.

This next essay, written by Jill, answers an almost identical question: "What are you most passionate about and why?"

✎ *Example: The "accidental" counselor*

Dawn is 16, a pastor's daughter who grew up in a strict Christian household. Although from the outside she appears happy, Dawn had actually attempted suicide the previous year. I met Dawn at a retreat organized by a network of churches for the spiritual enhancement of youth in the southeast. In early 20__ I was asked to join the Leadership Committee for the sponsoring organization and soon after was asked to counsel some of the girls. I hesitantly accepted, feeling inadequate to the task.

Dawn was one of my counselees at one retreat. We forged a strong connection and one night, when I saw she was close to tears, she confided her emotional turmoil, including her suicide attempt, which was still a secret outside her immediate family. She felt broken and had come to retreat to try to repair her relationship with God. I consoled her as best as I could, but my counselor's training had not prepared me to deal with attempted suicides, so I also recommended a counselor to help her heal from her past.

From that weekend, Dawn and I have remained in close contact, speaking or emailing once or twice a month. She went on to attend ____ College and her relationship with her family has greatly improved. My deepest passion lies in counseling and volunteering with young women like Dawn, who just want someone to talk to, someone who will take an interest in their lives, their trials and their triumphs. I've been lucky enough to have my past counselors take an interest in my life, and I am grateful that I can do the same for these younger girls now. My heart is focused on the lives of my counselees from prior youth retreats, my "little sisters."

✓ *What works*

In this essay the subject matter is totally unrelated to Jill's career goals but is no less compelling. The unexpected discovery of the writer's power to help heal a younger girl in turmoil and her commitment to remaining in touch adds the believability that this experience was not a one-shot deal.

Finally, this essay from Kate answers the prompt, "Describe a formative or significant event in your life and then explain how this event has influenced your subsequent thoughts and actions."

✒ *Example: Overcoming a traumatic event*

One afternoon shortly before my 10th birthday, I came home from school only to find my mother waiting for me on the front lawn, wearing her white wool coat. She never waited for me outside, and it wasn't even cold, so I was instantly alarmed: Something was very wrong. As I approached I saw she was crying. Years later, I still don't know how she managed to utter the devastating words, "There was a bad car accident, and your brother Ray is dead." Ray was 17.

In that instant I felt my childhood vanish. My world was no longer a safe place, where when people left the house to go somewhere they could be counted on to come home. I had nightmares, and during the day worried constantly that something would also happen to my parents, my sister, other relatives, or even me. My parents were naturally so consumed with grief that I was left much to my own devices to make sense of the tragedy. It was a lonely experience.

Fortunately, my maternal grandparents realized I needed extra attention and began picking me up Friday afternoons to spend the weekends with them at their house, about 20 miles away from where we lived. I'll never forget my grandfather saying, "Katie, tragedies happen to every family at some time or another. But you can and will survive the rough spots in life. Try to keep a smile on your face that reflects optimism from your own heart. Your smile will also help light up the hearts of everyone who meets you."

I didn't feel like smiling that much when I was back at home, given the gloomy environment, but I loved my grandfather so much that I tried to keep smiling for his sake. My weekends with my grandparents were filled with fun local outings to art fairs and parks, visits with their eclectic group of friends, who included authors and artists, and my grandfather's jokes. All these things helped me find and keep my smile.

In the 15 years since my brother died, I have worked steadily to overcome that undercurrent of worry about what other tragedies might lurk around the corner. And since my grandfather passed away five years ago, I have redoubled my efforts to being happy and to keeping that cheery smile on my face. I have read and gained immeasurably from many books on happiness, including Richard Carlson's *You Can Be Happy No Matter What* and Dennis Prager's *Happiness Is a Serious Problem*. It must be working, since I have friends and relatives who have called on me to offer advice and solace when they are also experiencing turmoil.

The smile I try to keep on my face may have been born of tragedy, but it is one that has grown to be authentically mine. It is also my grandfather's invaluable legacy to me.

✓ *What works*

Katie effectively draws an arc from a tragic significant event to her subsequent thoughts and actions, influenced primarily by her grandfather's emphasis on optimism. There is added poignancy and believability because Katie acknowledges that the process of being happy and optimistic has been the work of many yers, and has required bolstering from influential books. Mentioning that others sometimes call on her for emotional support also testifies to Katie's ability to have truly internalized her grandfather's lessons.

OPTIONAL ESSAY

"Should I write something for the optional essay?" This is a question many clients ask, especially if they don't have a weakness in their background that they'd like to explain. It's too bad when applicants feel that explaining away a weakness is the only reason to write the optional essay. In fact, using the optional to write about something positive, as opposed to addressing a low GPA, employment gap, or some other problem area on your record, has the potential to help make you more memorable and perhaps even remarkable to the adcoms.

First, a little advice for those who want to deal with a blemish on the record through the optional essay: Just as I advised handling a failure/setback through simple explanation, take the same tack for a profile weakness. State the circumstances surrounding the weakness simply and without indulging in overwrought apologies. Devote the majority of space to showing why that weakness does not reflect your true abilities. Direct the readers' attention to the steps you have taken to correct the weakness, if applicable. In the following example, notice how the writer shows what he did to turn an employment gap due to a family emergency into a success. His actions during this time show commitment, character and creativity:

✎ *Example: Caring for an ailing sister and family business*

In November 20__, my younger sister was diagnosed with a rare metabolic disorder and suddenly required ongoing medical attention and home care. As a result, my mother had to stop working in the family business, a holistic pharmacy which she had run with my father for more than 10 years. With sales already sliding at the pharmacy, my parents could not afford to hire a new staff person, so I quit my job as a marketing manager for _____ Health Systems to take her place, as well as to help care for my sister.

Unexpectedly, my help was required for nearly one year. When my sister's health improved enough for my mother to return to the business, finding full-time work in my field was considerably more difficult, as the economy was still in a major slump. This explains the 18-month gap outside of my field.

However, during this time I became active in a local marketing network-ing group and read many excellent books on marketing. Based on ideas I read in *The Tipping Point*, by Malcolm Gladwell, and *Duct Tape Market-ing*, by John Jantsch, I created new promotional ideas for our family busi-ness, set up its first web presence, and grew our community presence by helping to sponsor a community fair. These efforts helped to begin to reverse a steady decline in sales during the previous two years.

While I would much rather my sister never had gotten sick, my employ-ment gap provided me the ability to do the most important work of all: helping my family in crisis. In the process, I bolstered my professional knowledge and helped rebuild our family business.

Using the same strategy, the next writer mitigates the impact of a low GPA. Take special note of how she segregates her overall and major GPA from the overall GPA, showing that once she got serious about school in her sopho-more years, her academic abilities shone far more brightly:

✐ *Zapping the low GPA blues*

Coming from a small town in Michigan, where there were only 300 kids in my entire high school, I easily got swept up in the exciting variety of life at the University of Michigan. When I should have been studying, I was busy with the Women's Glee Club, broomball practices, and the Environmental Justice Group. Not surprisingly, all these distractions from my studies ensured that I would not qualify for other groups, such as the Dean's List.

Somehow, my first year GPA of 2.9 didn't faze me, but by the end of the first semester of my sophomore year it had dipped to 2.8, and I woke up to the reality that not only my scholarship, but my entire college educa-tion was on the line. I dropped all extracurricular activities except for the Glee Club, which I loved, and hit the books. While my overall GPA is a 3.2, my GPA from the second semester onward was a 3.6, and my GPA in my major of Economics was a 3.7.

My freshman immaturity was hardly original, but I hope the admissions committee will view my qualifications in light of my subsequent, steady

GPA and my GMAT of 700 as evidence that I will be able to perform well at ___ School of Business.

As useful as the optional essay is to reframe a weakness or employment gap, adcoms find it refreshing when applicants use this open space to write about something positive. Taking the opportunity to reveal something new about your life, abilities, or passions is another way to further distinguish yourself from other applicants. Sometimes, material that works for an achievement essay can also work for the optional. Here's how Scott did just that:

✐ *With a song in his heart*

I love jazz because there is a perfect tune to express what's in my heart; to perform it is incredibly powerful for me, and if I do it right, for the audience also. But it has taken many years for me to develop this art. Six years ago, I moved to San Francisco to pursue jazz more fully. I began singing with a jazz pianist and was inspired by the seemingly effortless, passionate performances of greats such as Dee Dee Bridgewater. Yet my first open mic at The Mint was a disaster. Unable to hear myself given the poor sound system, I sang the entire song off-key to the excruciating dismay of the diners. After being ushered off stage, the pianist told me not to bother with music anymore. But I attended another session the next day.

I had much to learn, including improving my vocal technique, calming my nerves, coping with my imperfect hearing, and understanding that as a vocalist I was also a bandleader. After two years and many public failures, I studied jazz theory and ear training. I added 20-25 hours of rehearsal per week and continued to brave open mics and guest appearances. Eventually, my hard work transformed me from hack to musician. My vocal coach improved my technique and taught me to brand myself as a unique cross between Tony Bennett's elegance and Dee Dee Bridgewater's passion, through the right retro attire, repertoire and stage persona. While the performance experience was invaluable, the music theory, ear training and coaching accelerated my growth and bolstered my confidence. At a recent performance for 500 guests at the resplendent Adrianna Ballroom in Portland, Oregon, I entertained the crowd with a mix of ballads and swing tunes for three hours over dinner and swing dancing while leading a four-piece band through visual cues. After danc-

ing the night away, several attendees asked about future performances—
I have come a long way since The Mint.

It's easy to see how an optional essay like this could help the adcoms remember Scott not as just another finance/entrepreneur/marketing careerist, but as "the jazz singer."

The following essay is also one that could work as either an achievement-themed essay or an optional. This was written in response to the prompt, "Tell us about yourself and your personal interests. The goal of this essay is to get a sense of who you are rather than what you have achieved professionally." When deciding whether an essay that you wrote as an achievement essay might work as an optional for another school, or vice-versa, keep in mind the values of the school and the balance of material in your essay packages.

✐ The punching bag

Standing amongst my colleagues at the company holiday party, I noticed some of my peers eyeing a small red punching bag in the corner of the room. Before I knew it, the group began betting on who was the strongest person at the event. When all bets were placed, each man took a turn punching the bag. Eventually, someone called for me to participate. As one of two women in my investment banking analyst class, some thought I would decline the invitation. Instead, I headed to the front of the line, slipped off my high heels and punched the bag with all my might. The room fell silent. To everyone's surprise, I managed to out-score my boss and most of the other favorites in the group. Blushing but proud, I put my heels back on and resumed chatting with a group of friends.

In the spirit of full disclosure, I have a black belt in karate, played collegiate athletics and studied boxing. As such, I had a distinct and unknown advantage. Furthermore, I love challenges and was thrilled to compete with "the boys." Growing up as an athlete with asthma, I never let my breathing difficulties stop me from pursuing my athletic goals. Each practice was a challenge that I both accepted and enjoyed as I pursued my passion for team athletics. This desire to take on challenges has been a recurring theme in my life and played a formative role in shaping my identity.

For example, during the first day of practice on Columbia's volleyball team I was told that we were in desperate need of defensive players. Eager to help the team and accept the challenge of learning a new position, I volunteered to switch from offense to defense. This transition required long hours in the gym honing my defensive skills. After a few days in the new role I realized that I needed to adjust not only my skills, but also my leadership style for the new position.

As the defensive specialist, I could no longer rally the team by scoring decisive points. Rather, I was expected to lead by providing consistency and support in the back row. I took advantage of my newfound vantage point overlooking the entire court to direct communication among my teammates, who began to look to me to coordinate our defensive strategies. I learned that people do not need to be on the front line to lead effectively, a lesson that has helped me lead teams as an analyst at a large investment bank.

I hope this treasure trove of examples will help you expand your vision of what can work beautifully in these specific essay questions you may face. In the next chapter, let's look at creating a terrific MBA applicant resume.

The Bottom Line

→ **MAP out your essays** by including elements that reveal your **M**otivations, **A**spirations and **P**erspiration – the efforts you have made that prove dedication to your goal.

→ **Demonstrate leadership** in essays through active verbs (listening, directing, organizing, etc.) and specifying how you met challenges.

→ **Distinguish between short- and long-term goals.** List milestones or your ideal position you would like to achieve at each stage as well as the industry where you envision yourself in both stages.

→ **Name specific classes, professors, programs and internship opportunities** when addressing the "Why Our School?" part of the goals essay.

→ **Own your mistakes** in a "failure" or "setback" essay. **Prove you have learned** from the mistake by demonstrating what you do differently now to avoid repeating them.

→ **Go deep** when answering the "personal influences" or "what matters most to you and why" questions. Be specific about who or what influenced you and **show how you integrate those values** in your life today.

→ **Capitalize on the optional essay** as an opportunity to reveal something unexpected about your personality or nonwork-related skills or experiences. Address weaknesses as succinctly as possible, focusing on why the weakness doesn't exist anymore.

13 Rules for Resumes that Rock

As everybody knows, you can only make *one* first impression. Because adcom members often look at your resume before they view anything else in your application, it is critical that you do everything in your power to ensure that this first impression is as robust as possible. Think of your resume as your entire candidacy encapsulated on one page (two at most), and be mindful that often, your resume won't receive more than a thirty-second glance. It's no easy feat to condense your most salient career achievements on a single page, but you can do it.

Here are my rules for creating a dynamic and powerful resume that will reward every second of the adcom member's viewing time, a resume whose every line will add stature to your candidacy:

Your goal is to create a winning MBA applicant resume, not a job resume

Resumes for employment might naturally include industry-specific or technical lingo and a list of software or other technical programs that you know. These have no place in an MBA application resume, whose sole purpose is to provide a meaningful snapshot of your career achievements and progression. It will also show that your work and other experiences are consistent with your stated goals.

> **1** Limit resumes to one page, unless you have more than ten years' work experience.

Many schools will accept two-page resumes. However, at conferences of graduate school admissions consultants and school admissions staff that I attended, there was consistent overwhelming preference among adcom members at the top-20 schools for one-page resumes. With so much material to read, they appreciate your brevity. Is a two-page resume a deal-breaker? No, but unless you have more than a decade of professional experience under your belt or some other superlative achievements that simply demand that extra page, keep it short and sweet --one page.

② **Place a qualifications summary at the top of your resume.**

This qualifications summary serves as a headline for your resume, drawing attention to your most impressive qualifications and achievements. The qualifications summary is not an "objectives" summary, which is irrelevant in an MBA resume. Too often, though, even qualifications summaries are stuffed with boring verbiage that can make a reader's eyes glaze over. Done right, however, visually appealing headlines written in concise text boxes, bullet points, bold text or similar style will "strike readers immediately with illustrations of your exceptional impact, enticing them to read more about you out of interest, not out of obligation," observes Jennifer Bloom, Accepted.com editor and Certified Professional Resume Writer.

Jennifer suggests that you write the rest of your resume first, because when you are satisfied with that, it will be easier to pick out your strongest assets for the summary headline. Depending on the length of your resume and the space you have to work with, Jennifer recommends choosing among the following for the qualifications summary:

- ☑ A short personality summary and/or career history.

- ☑ Achievement highlights.

- ☑ Anything notable in your past that is relevant to the program you are applying for. This is especially useful for projects and impacts that occurred further in the past and would otherwise be buried near the end of the résumé.

Some specific examples of achievements worth noting in a qualifications summary might include:

- ☑ If you earned three promotions in two years – four years in advance of the traditional path for your company.

☑   If you initiated and successfully led a new venture from within your organization.

☑   If you feel you have a unique attribute that will differentiate you from all the other applicants:

Don't repeat the exact same wording in a summary as in the resume itself. If you highlight a project from your current work in two lines in the Qualifications Summary, for example, use only one line – and perhaps different statistics about it – to summarize it in the Professional Experience section. While there are no rules about how the summary should look, it should ideally appear as a set of minisections, each boasting of an accomplishment in your education, career or extracurricular activities.

Despite the potential impact of a well done qualifications summary, I still recommend that if adding it will make your resume spill over to a second page and you have less than a decade of work experience, leave it out.

③ Focus on impact and achievements, not responsibilities.

Top business school adcoms are looking for career progression. This means that a list of basic job descriptions just won't cut it. One of the most common resume errors I see is wasting a bullet point describing job responsibilities in terms that basically duplicate a job title. If you are an analyst, you don't need to say that you "analyze problems and develop optimal solutions." That's what analysts do. If you are a consultant, you don't need to write that you "consult with clients on improving their business." That's what consultants do. Don't bore your reader by repeating the obvious and writing in terms that make you sound like every other candidate with a similar title.

Your job title is not what will distinguish you. Nor will the description of your responsibilities. Instead, what will distinguish you is *what you achieved when you held that title*. The best way to highlight the impact you have made in that job is to do the following:

(4) **Quantify your impact on the organizations you've worked for with specifics.**

Include details such as: how much or by what percentage you reduced expenses, how many people were on the team that you supervised, how much or by what percentage you increased sales, and the like. Don't say, "Developed e-commerce plan that was selected for implementation" when you mean "Designed $5 million e-commerce strategy that increased revenues by 12% and attracted 6 new clients." Don't use a vague phrase such as "led a team" when in fact you led a six-person team responsible for the rollout of a new product that brought in $300,000 in six months, or that you led a ten-person cross-functional team that redesigned and implemented a new company website that increased page views by more than 56%. If you work for a private company and can't disclose revenue figures, refer to *percentage* increases or improvements, or cite the improved industry *ranking* of the organization's product or performance as a result of your contribution.

(5) **Give your most recent professional experience the most attention.**

Limit the number of bullet points describing your early entry-level roles to no more than two bullet points. For instance, if you were promoted from an entry-level programming position with your company, then you don't even need to dedicate a separate line to describe that first role. Instead, devote your precious resume real estate to positions where you had the greatest impact. In most cases, this will involve your current position, which will deserve the most space. To stay within the preferred one-page format, try to limit your current or most recent position to four bulleted accomplishments. Following this format, you can impress the reader by describing the fast pace of promotion from your early positions in a line of the job description, like this:

Team Lead, IT Consulting Company   2008-Present

Twice promoted from Analyst (2007-2008) to Senior Analyst (2008) and then Team Lead in record 12 months, a full 4 times faster than the average rate of promotion.

What if you have recently changed jobs and haven't had yet been able to show much career progression or initiative but have some killer accomplishments in a previous position? If this is your situation, which is a common one, by all means devote more bullet points to demonstrating what you achieved in a prior position. Ideally, you will not have to reach back more than a year in your employment history to do this.

6 Don't list each promotion as if it represents a new position at a new employer.

If one position has allowed you significant leadership opportunities and impact or you have been in your current role for several years, it might be impossible to detail what you consider your major accomplishments in just four bullet points. However, it's a mistake to list each promotion as if it is a new position with a new company. Jennifer observes, "Listing promotions as if they are new positions actually *detracts* from the attention that the promotion gets. Instead, I advise applicants to list the company name and total dates of employment at the top, followed by a list of each role with its bullets beneath that (next to the job title in parentheses can be listed the dates of that individual position)."

A breakdown of your promotions/achievements at a single company might look like this:

Private Equity Associate, PE Firm   2008-Present

Lines of job description here…

Leadership Accomplishments Include:

- First point
- Second point
- Third point
- Fourth point

Financial Impacts Include:

- First point
- Second point
- Third point
- Fourth point

Keep in mind that the majority – if not all – of those bullet points should include quantifiable impact that you had on the organization. Breaking up a bulk of text with numbers and section headings makes the entire document more compelling.

(7) Emphasize leadership at every opportunity.

Leadership is a broad term that covers a lot of territory and can be manifested in many ways. You can demonstrate leadership not only by taking charge of an engagement or project, but also by seizing the initiative to add value to your organization. This can mean recruiting peers and staff to get buy-in on an idea or project or to work together to achieve a goal. When you think about leadership in this more expansive way, you will invariably find that you have more examples of it than you thought. On your resume, try to frame your leadership triumphs in terms of how they benefited the organization you worked for.

(8) Leave high school back in high school.

Don't bother including your high school activities, unless you had truly extraordinary achievements, such as winning a prestigious national award or something else dazzling for someone that young.

(9) Place your educational information after your work experience.

Your resume should present your experiences with your most prominent and impressive experiences first. That means that if you have more than two years of work experience, put your education information after work experience. Do not waste space by including GPA, GMAT, SAT or other statistics. The schools will have all that information on your application.

(10) Use verbs to begin every bullet-pointed item.

Verbs make you sound like a dynamic individual who is always ready for action. Don't say, "Responsible for the development of inventory-control system" when you can say "Developed inventory-control system." Additionally, using verbs to begin your bullet-pointed lists saves words and will strengthen the tone and content of your resume throughout. Look for opportunities to include strong cooperation-laden verbs, such as *assist*, *contribute*, *support*, or *provide*.

 Design your resume to be user friendly.

The skillful use of understated design can result in an eye-catching resume that projects a sophisticated, successful image. Avoid fussy typefaces -- nothing in script or with squiggles. Stick with a conservative style, and go easy on the busy eyes of the adcom members – no smaller than a 10-point font size. In her Accepted.com Admissions Almanac blog titled *Admissions Resume: What to Include*, Jennifer offers this excellent advice:

> "To ensure that your document is easy to read and keeps the admissions officer's attention, include ample white space. To add some white space above each position in Microsoft Word, highlight the title line of each row (hold the Ctrl button down as you click to keep them all highlighted), then click on Format, Paragraph, then in the Spacing Before box try at least 4 pt. (if you have more space left on the page at the end you can go to 6 pt.). Do the same Ctrl highlighting for the bullet points throughout the document and try 2 pt. or 3 pt. spacing before each of those lines."

 Include notable extras.

These include honors, publications, presentations, patents, professional licenses or certifications, and relevant volunteer experiences. These extras could convince the adcom to invite you in for an interview. Don't go overboard, however. If you're one of those people who has been a research assistant on a dozen projects or received honors since elementary school, you'll have to select judiciously to include what is truly most impressive. Your mother may still love to brag that you were Honor Student of the Month in junior high school, but leave those bragging rights to her.

 Proofread and edit mercilessly.

Reduce fluff and make every word count. Use style check and spell check (*even though ewe no spell Czech cannot catch awl errors*). Have a friend or a professional editor review your resume for errors you may have missed.

Now that you know what you *should* do . . . make sure you also avoid:

8 Resume Blunders

(1) **Making things up.**

This includes inflating your accomplishments, your level of responsibility, employment dates, or your skills. Besides being dishonest, your resume reviewer may find out if he or she decides to follow up on one of your references or does a background check. In that case, you're toast.

(2) **Inflating your resume into an autobiography.**

Your resume will include minimal biographical information, but its primary purpose is to focus on aspects of your life and career that make you an ideal b-school candidate and that address a potential employer's needs.

(3) **Providing personal or irrelevant information.**

That means no SAT or GMAT scores, no GPA, no high school education, and no references. The school will have all of that information from other parts of your application. Personal data, including marital status, age, height/weight, race, religion, or any other non-work-related information is also a no-no. If you want to let the employer know that you're from a minority group without adding a personal data section, add a Memberships section and include the name of community organizations you belong to, for example, the "South Asian Business Alliance of Ohio." This will tell the adcom members what groups you identify with in a more subtle way.

(4) **Including a separate "objective" line at the beginning of your resume.**

This is a waste of valuable space and irrelevant in MBA application resumes. Instead, if space permits, write a qualifications summary (discussed above).

(5) Including articles or pronouns.

Article such as "the" or "a" and pronouns such as "I" waste precious space, detract from resume impact and reduce professionalism.

(6) Overusing common action words.

It's easy to overwork action words such as "led" or "developed." Think outside that little verb box and consider terms such as "accelerated," "delivered," "established," "implemented," "initiated" or "reengineered."

(7) Claiming that you are "dynamic," a "self-starter," or other clichéd terms.

"Show, don't tell" remains a cardinal rule of writing. Instead of claiming that you are dynamic or a self-starter, show that you personify these qualities by including the salient aspects of your experience in the details of your resume.

(8) Forgetting dates.

Functional resumes should include dates of employment, even if they're only included at the end.

Avoiding these pitfalls will help you achieve a resume that shines the light on your achievements and points to your future potential – and is easy on the eyes, too. The adcom members will thank you for it.

Examples

Look at the two sample resumes that follow[7]. Notice how both applicants followed all the rules outlined above and avoided the pitfalls. As you craft your own MBA application resume, refer back to this chapter and to these samples, which you might want to use as a template.

Resume 1 – Finance Background (with qualifications summary)

Jane Jones

4 Crest Road Manchester, New Hampshire
Mobile: xxx-200-0000 Email: jane.jones@gmail.com

Qualifications Summary

Accomplished **Banking Professional** with international background and **5 years of finance experience** in credit, financial, and risk analysis plus portfolio risk management. Areas of expertise include banking, mortgage insurance, real estate, and consumer credit risk. Excellent team player who collaborates well with peers and executives.

Analytical and Quick Thinking: Directed and prepared quarterly reporting and analysis of company's $15 billion portfolio – role usually filled by Risk Reporting Manager. Summarized portfolio quality and performance and directed executive management toward more profitable segments. Reduced report production time by 50%.

Interpersonal Skills: Guided executive management of a top-5 U.S. bank to change its lending practices at a national level and met with executive management of borrowing institutions to assess their overall risk profile.

Quantitative Ability: Managed the credit risk of a $3 billion mortgage portfolio through analysis of portfolio and overall industry performance, outperforming industry benchmarks by 30% and maintaining overall profitability.
Entrepreneurial: Established a new process to obtain regulatory financial data six weeks earlier than previously available – only 2 weeks after the quarter's close – allowing better decision making by management and peers.

---

7   Although the resumes appear here on multiple pages they fit well into a standard U.S. 8.5 x 11" sheet of paper. If you would like to see how they look please visit http://www.accepted.com/mafs/resume1 and http://www.accepted.com/mafs/resume2.

Professional Experience

Sr. Risk Analyst/Risk Analyst, Barclay's Capital (Chicago, USA)
June 20__ - June 20__

- Analyzed portfolio/overall industry performance and managed the credit risk of a $3 billion mortgage portfolio, outperforming industry benchmarks by 30% and maintaining overall profitability despite severe market downturn.
- Priced and structured credit-default insurance coverage for mortgage loan portfolios to achieve regulatory-capital and risk management objectives of client financial institutions. Increased insured portfolio by 40%.
- Directed and prepared quarterly reporting and analysis of company's $15 billion portfolio: summarized portfolio quality, performance, and profitability to better advise executive management in their decision-making process.
- Developed strategies and protocols for increasing operational efficiency between Risk Management and other departments, reducing premium delivery time by 93%.

Credit Analyst, Credit Suisse Group (Chicago, USA)
August 20__ - June 20__

- Prepared credit analyses of financial institutions and recommended actions to manage the bank's credit risk exposure to borrowing institutions, which ranged from community banks to large European banks. Researched and analyzed economic, legal, and political trends affecting American and European banking industries.
- Established a new process to obtain regulatory financial data six weeks earlier, locating bad assets on balance sheets of borrowing banks just two weeks after their quarterly closings and positioning FHLB to respond quickly.
- Monitored value of collateral (mortgages, securities) and assisted in monitoring credit risk of the Bank's loan and investment portfolio, including mortgage-backed securities (RMBS, ABS), treasury and corporate bonds.
- Examined borrowing institutions' credit guidelines, loan files, and collection practices then guided their executive management in such matters as increasing capital adequacy ratios to reduce their risk profiles.

Fixed Income/Operations Intern, Southern Asset Management, L.P. (Nashville, TN)
June 20__- December 20__

- Assisted portfolio managers with pricing and credit analysis of Treasury, corporate bonds, and asset-backed securities. Reduced costs of trade confirmation by 75% by implementing electronic trade confirmation

Education

Carroll School of Management, Boston College (Boston, MA)
May 20__
- Bachelor of Arts in Economics and Corporate Reporting and Analysis
- President's List, Dean's List, Omicron Delta Epsilon,
  Beta Gamma Sigma

Relevant Involvements Include:
- Treasurer, Finance Academy
- Research Team Member, Smart Woman Securities

Other Skills and interests
- Fluency in Spanish, English, working knowledge of French
- Microsoft Excel, Access, Word, PowerPoint, and Outlook;
  Bloomberg; SQL
- Play guitar, compose music, avid yoga practitioner

Resume 2 – Business Development Background (without qualifications summary)

RAHUL VERMA

23 Paddington Court, Tunbridge Wells, United Kingdom, TN1 9QJ
(+44) 0189287729, rverma@gmail.com

EXPERIENCE

Saxon Consulting Group 20__ – Present
(Cape Town, South Africa) Senior Consultant (20__ – Present)

Leadership Impact

- Promoted from Associate Consultant to Senior Consultant in less than two years based on high performance results and involvement in leadership roles.
- Produced marketing materials to attract prospective clients, resulting in 2 client engagements.
- Managed teams of up to five associates for hospital clients of multi-facility health systems and specialized facilities.

- Increased profitability by 20% across 5 projects by using historical data to estimate project revenue, goals and project staffing.
- Supervised and evaluated career development of 15 associates and co-led mentorship program.
- Designed and led quarterly training module providing new hires a clinical overview of fundamental medical services and procedures.

Financial Impact

- Generated $4 MM (US) in new contracts with 3 hospitals for secure electronic patient record system.
- Generated $10MM (US) in savings for hospital clients by providing financial operations and revenue cycle recommendations.
- Increased profitability by 20% across 5 projects by using historical data to estimate project revenue, goals and project staffing.

EDUCATION

Cambridge University, St. Catharine's College 20__ – 20__
Bachelor of Science, Finance; Minor in Marketing
Vice President: Indian Students Association; Member: Omega Phi Alpha Service Organization

Griffith University, *Study Abroad Program* Brisbane, Australia 20__
Coursework in Portfolio Management and International Business Finance

VOLUNTEER EXPERIENCE/INTERESTS

Saxon Consulting Group Sustainability Lead 20__ - 20__

Organized fundraiser for 200+ to benefit Family House, housing for families of seriously ill children receiving treatment at Somerset Hospital; raised $23,000.

- Led 15 co-workers in renovating Home Away from Homelessness headquarters, an organization dedicated to providing a safe place for displaced youth to interact away from shelters.

Room To Read Volunteer, Cape Town, South Africa 20__ – Present

- Recruited 4 local business to help sponsor the Room to Read initiative, offering tutoring to local children.

PERSONAL INTERESTS

Photography, reading, outdoor activities, and traveling; recent trips include Kenya and Tanzania

The Bottom Line ⟵┄┄┄┄┄┄┄┄┄┄┄┄┄

→ **Focus on career progression in your** MBA application resume. Highlight career impact with specific, quantified achievements.

→ **Break up large chunks of text** with data and section headings to underscore career growth.

→ **Frame leadership triumphs** in terms of *how* they benefited the organization you worked for.

→ **Begin bullet-pointed lines with action verbs** to emphasize leadership.

→ **Avoid clichés, exaggeration and irrelevant information.**

┄┄┄┄┄┄┄┄┄┄┄┄┄┄┄┄┄┄┄┄┄┄┄┄┄┄┄┄┄⟶

Chapter 8

How to Gather Fabulous Letters of Recommendation

Gathering strong Letters of Recommendation (LORs) may strike you as one of the more annoying details of your MBA application and possibly even redundant. Haven't you already proven in your essays and through your stellar resume how amazingly focused, smart, diverse and dedicated you are to earning your MBA? You may think so, but the adcoms want even *more* proof. So, even if you are incubating a case of Application Season Fatigue Syndrome (not yet listed in the annals of medical literature), take a deep breath and reach back for that final burst of energy you still need, because LORs are read carefully by adcoms and can be highly influential to the acceptance process.

What do LORs accomplish?

☑ *Validate claims.* Because they are written by a third party, they affirm that what you claim about yourself in your essays is true.

☑ *Reveal new and distinct qualifications.* They provide an opportunity to showcase additional managerial or leadership experiences or exemplary characteristics that you didn't have room to discuss in your essays.

☑ *Counteract a weakness.* For example, if you're a quant jock, you should look for someone who can talk up your communication skills. Conversely, if you come from a nontraditional professional background, you should find a recommender who can testify to your quantitative and analytical skills.

☑ *Develop a fuller picture of you.* Since they offer a complementary (and complimentary) perspective about your leadership, integrity, and other characteristics, LORs round out your profile beyond the academic and what you managed to convey in your essays. Through third-party validation, they confirm that you are a well-rounded person of good character who can fit well with the school and its environment.

In fact, when the adcom wrestles between extending an offer to two otherwise equally qualified candidates, a stellar LOR can tip those precariously balanced scales in your favor. Conversely, lackluster LORs that fail to add any new insights and lack enthusiasm can doom your application.

Who should write your recommendations?

There are probably only a few people who are qualified to do justice to these letters, yet choosing the right candidates is vital. Here's how to choose among potential recommenders and make their job easier.

Effective letters of recommendation highlight and amplify your leadership, teamwork, organizational and communication skills. They offer examples of the value you have brought to an organization. This means that managers, supervisors and professional mentors are ideal candidates for this task. Having supervised you over a period of time and seen you in a variety of situations, they can respond knowledgably to most, if not all, of the questions that schools raise. LOR forms ask recommenders to answer a range of questions, such as how you stand out from others in a similar capacity and in what ways you have had an impact on your organization. They also ask for assessments about your leadership experiences and potential, including attributes such as intelligence, creativity, focus, integrity and communication skills. They may even ask to rate your sense of humor.

Aside from discussing your strengths, recommenders are also asked to assess your weaknesses and what you have done to remedy them. Consequently you need recommenders who really know not only about your proven abilities and talents, but also about areas where you can improve and do so without drawing attention to or magnifying any weaknesses that you do have. (Hint: This means your mother is out of the running as a recommender – even if she is your boss!)

What if I can't ask my current manager?

A current or recent manager, supervisor or other department head would be ideal, but if you need to keep your MBA application hush-hush, ask a former supervisor as long as he or she did not supervise you more than three years ago. You should also get someone who can speak about your skills and abilities *now*, such as a team lead or manager of another department where you currently work. Recruiting a recommender who knows you well and cares about you and your plans will result in a far more effective LOR than getting someone in the company with a high title who barely knows you to sign off on a letter about you.

What if I'm self-employed?

If you run your own company, good recommender options include a partner, consultant, major client, vendor, supplier, attorney, accountant, or board member, if applicable. Whomever you choose should have a longstanding relationship with you (at least two years) during which you've had opportunities to display your integrity, professionalism and other strengths. Under no circumstances should you ask a relative (especially one who shares your last name) to write your LOR, even if you work in a family business. If you work in a nontraditional, nonbusiness environment, make sure that at least one of your recommenders can speak to your business acumen and management potential.

Asking for LORs – tools to make your recommender's job easier

Writing a meaningful and beneficial LOR will take at a minimum one to two hours of a recommender's time, which is a lot to ask of an already busy person. Ask for a brief meeting with your hoped-for recommender, explaining your plans for graduate study and why you are applying to the MBA programs that you have chosen. Explain what you need the LOR to accomplish for you, including the addition of new, distinct details about your work experience and management potential that will further burnish your image with the adcoms. Offer tangible information that will make her job easier, including your essays. Then ask if she feels she is the right person for the job. If she doesn't feel she can endorse you enthusiastically or cannot give the letter the time it requires, she can politely decline, and you can move on to the next possible recommender.

Once you have recommenders lined up, give them the tools they need to get the job done. These will include:

☑ A brief overview of how you are trying to position yourself with the school.

☑ A resume.

☑ Copies of each LOR form, with basic data already filled in.

☑ Timeline to submit the LOR to meet the school's deadline. If applicable, stamped and addressed envelopes.

☑ A list of experiences, anecdotes or other stories that you would like mentioned. These should be chosen with an eye toward strengthening any weaknesses in your application. As much as possible, the stories you suggest should be different from those already discussed in your essays, though it would be natural to mention a very significant achievement in both an LOR and an essay. A brief summary of the target schools' values, organized by school.

☑ Copies of relevant work evaluations.

☑ Copies of your essays, if you already have essay drafts.

Two sample LORs

Example 1: Srikanth

Srikanth is a 31-year-old working in the IT industry. He graduated from one of India's most prestigious engineering colleges with a degree in computer engineering, and he's worked for two computer software start-ups, one in India and one in the United States. He created a new software tool at one company which is under review for a patent and which has begun to create a strong revenue stream for the company. Srikanth's LOR will have to combat two weaknesses: being a member of an overrepresented applicant pool, and his much stronger quant scores versus communication scores on the GMAT. This LOR is written based on Wharton's form for 2011.

1 How long have you known the applicant and describe your relationship to the applicant?

I hired Srikanth three years ago to join our start-up company, MedSolutions. Although he was hired as a software engineer, Srikanth's talents and contributions to the company led me to promote him to Senior Engineer in only one year. I work with him on a regular basis, reviewing the progress of various software solutions we are selling and developing. I try to have lunch or coffee with Srikanth once a week, since he is now the team lead for the other five software engineers in my employ and these meetings help keep me apprised of both problems and new ideas that come from the software development side of things. As the president and co-founder of the company, I remain Srikanth's supervisor and am glad he remains on our team.

 2 Provide an example of constructive feedback you have provided to the applicant. How did the applicant receive this feedback and what efforts did the applicant make to address the concern?

While Srikanth has always communicated well with co-workers, customers and vendors, his accent is strong, and he has been hesitant to speak to larger groups. When I first asked him to give a presentation at a healthcare tradeshow last year about a software solution that he helped devise, I saw that he was very uncomfortable with the idea. I suggested to Srikanth that he work to strengthen his English speaking skills and join Toastmasters. While his lack of English fluency had not yet hurt him professionally, I felt it would if he didn't take steps to address it. Srikanth seemed relieved to have a path to deal with this weakness, and he began attending a local Toastmasters group regularly. By the time the trade show rolled around three months later, Srikanth was willing to give the presentation, and his speaking abilities and comfort level improved. At my suggestion, he is also enrolled in an accent remediation program.

 3 Please provide an example of a time when the applicant was particularly successful at interacting with others in a team (employees, peers, managers, etc.); how was the applicant successful? How does the applicant compare to his/her peers in this dimension?

Srikanth's workgroup has five other software engineers, and all are very focused and even professionally competitive to varying degrees. Six months ago, the group had fallen two weeks behind schedule in delivering a product for a medical records company, and the client was unhappy. There was frustration and tension in the group over the delay and a temptation to find fault with others. As the team lead, Srikanth was willing to just listen to the venting, which helped defuse the tension. He was able to redirect attention and energy toward finding solutions now rather than dwelling on what was or might have been. I believe that his maturity and leadership in this situation kept the project from losing more momentum and the team from getting bogged down in needless recriminations. This is one reason why I promoted Srikanth more quickly than some of his peers, and he continues to display not only hard work but mature perspective that has made him a leader in the company.

Additionally, when Srikanth saw the potential for this same product to be customized for other healthcare clients, he devoted many hours to demonstrating its potential for other uses. His presentation to me and the company COO was persuasive enough that we gave him the green light to pick two other engineers to work on the customization project with him. We plan to file a patent on this product, and it is already bringing us new business that I would estimate to have been worth at least $50,000 in the last three months alone.

These are two reasons why I find that Srikanth consistently performs at a level equal to or exceeding that of his peers, particularly in terms of leadership, taking initiative, and suggesting new ideas to expand our market share with additional product ideas.

 4 Provide an example of a time when the applicant did not meet expectations. What was the outcome? How did s/he handle the setback?

About two years ago, one client complained about poor customer support with a product. Srikanth had been her contact. While this client was high-maintenance, I felt that Srikanth was not as patient in his explanations as he could have or should have been. I also suspect that he took her brusque manner as a personal insult, which I doubt that it was. She was so upset over the incident that she cancelled an order for additional products worth about $10,000. I told Srikanth about the cancelled order, and we spoke about alternate ways the situation could have been handled. To his credit, he did not become defensive and acknowledged his need to become more patient with certain customers. He has since read a few books on working with difficult people and has worked on active listening and other tools to deal more successfully with situations like this. This situation was a springboard from which he has grown into a more mature and able leader. In fact, some months later the same customer reinstated her order.

5 How has the applicant's career progressed over the time that you have known him/her? How does this growth compare to his/her peer group? Please describe the peer group to which you are comparing this applicant.

When Srikanth first arrived, he was a good and capable software engineer who was excited by the opportunity to join a start-up, despite the risks. As mentioned above, his leadership skills and ability to see the company perspective as a whole, and not just the technical aspects of our work, led me to promote him quickly, a decision that has benefitted the company greatly. His ability to accept constructive criticism and take it as an opportunity to grow professionally have continued to impress me and show that he is head and shoulders above his peers. All the engineers are in their late 20s or early 30s, and all are competitive. But Srikanth has chosen to take the mindset of a company stakeholder rather than just than an employee. As one example, he frequently sends me links to articles on marketing for small businesses or start-ups, with notes about how we could borrow some of those ideas for MedSolutions.

Srikanth continues to grow in his sense of entrepreneurial energy on behalf of the company. In fact, in the last year he joined an entrepreneurial networking association on behalf of MedSolutions and has also organized guest speakers at the group's meetings. All these qualities and the steady growth in his performance prove to me that he is true management material.

6 Provide any additional comments you think would assist the Admissions Committee in making its decision.

I would be very sorry to lose Srikanth as an employee if he left my company for another firm, but I would be gratified to know that I lost him to Wharton. He is head and shoulders above most engineers in terms of his ability to see the company perspective as a whole and not just the technical aspects of our work. His leadership and initiative are comparable to the best MBAs I have worked with not only at my firm, but in my previous work at Microsoft. With an MBA of my own from Duke, I appreciate how valuable this education will be to his future prospects, and I would welcome him back to MedSolutions after he completes his MBA.

Srikanth has told me that in the future he'd like to run his own software development company focused on solutions for the healthcare industry, and his three years with MedSolutions have opened his eyes to the potential for growth in this rapidly changing field. I am convinced that his enthusiasm for this field is sincere and that with more experience and an MBA education, he has the potential to realize this goal.

✓ *What works*

Srikanth's LOR is effective because it includes specific examples that illustrate his team spirit, entrepreneurial drive, leadership, and generosity of spirit. While it mentioned his weakness as a public speaker, the recommender mitigated this weakness by noting how Srikanth had already worked to overcome it. Also note how the recommender made sure to mention that he himself has an MBA from another top school, which signals to the adcom that he understands to a large extent what they are looking for in a candidate.

Example 2: Min

Min is a 27-year-old Chinese-American who worked for JP Morgan Chase until her job was eliminated during a restructuring. This LOR was written by her direct supervisor at the bank very shortly after her job loss. Min's profile through her work history, essays and GMAT show her to be a bit of a quant jock, a weakness that her recommender keeps in mind when she writes this letter of support, which is based on Columbia's 2011 LOR form. Note how the recommender helps fight the stereotype with her answer to the last question.

 What is your relationship to and how long have you known the applicant? Is this person still employed by your organization? If not, when did he/she depart?

Min reported directly to me in her role as a junior analyst at JP Morgan for two years, until her position was cut during a recent company restructuring. I argued with higher management to keep her, given her talent and potential, but was overruled, and Min was let go two months ago. I have worked with dozens of such young analysts in my 15 years in this industry, and I recognized in Min a person who was not only smart and a very hard worker, but a person of character whom I was proud to know and happy to work with. She was an asset to the company, and I have missed her since she has been gone.

 Please provide a short list of adjectives describing the applicant's strengths, and please compare the applicant's performance to that of his or her peers.

The adjectives that come to mind when I think of Min are: hardworking, brainy, focused, enthusiastic, driven and resilient.

While no one was ever hired at JP Morgan who lacked intelligence (even when nepotism was involved from time to time in hiring decisions), a certain baseline of smarts and especially a facility with numbers was required to last here for more than one day. But Min's love of finance, numbers, and for researching and financial forecasting was palpable. Additionally, I found her intelligence and her maturity to have been on par with analysts several years her senior. For example, sometimes younger analysts are so eager to show results that they don't take the time to double-check their numbers or research. Min was mature and patient enough to take that extra step and double-check her work before presenting it to me. Consequently, it was far more accurate than the work of analysts with similar experience.

In addition to her outstanding performance with number crunching, I found Min's cheerful disposition especially refreshing in an environment that is so often stressful. Even when the heat was on, Min did not show the strain in the way that one would have understood and expected. She never became short-tempered, made biting comments, or became in other ways difficult, even while working under strained circumstances.

 Please compare the applicant's performance to that of his/her peers. Does the applicant have the potential to become a senior manager?

In the two years that Min worked under me, I saw very exciting growth and potential for significant managerial responsibilities. While she was first hired to assist me and other senior analysts with forecasting research, her learning curve was so fast that within one year I was confident enough to give her higher level work. In fact, when one senior analyst had to take an extended medical leave, I recommended that Min replace her on a team of more senior analysts who were working on financial forecasting work that involved using spreadsheet and statistical software packages to help analyze data. Min performed very well with the team and in my opinion should have been promoted based on that performance alone.

 4 How effective are the applicant's interpersonal skills in working with peers, supervisors, and subordinates?

Min was highly respected by her peers and superiors. Sometimes I sensed that she was a just a bit frustrated when working with junior analysts who didn't work or think as fast as she did, but she still managed to patiently answer the same questions repeatedly from another junior analyst about a research project they were working on together. Like many others from an Asian culture, Min is by nature more quiet, but didn't let her natural reticence keep her from communicating clearly and in a collegial manner with others in the department.

 5 How does the applicant accept constructive criticism?

Min is very driven to succeed and has a bit of a perfectionist streak. I sensed that as much as she achieved at work, she felt it was never enough. I spoke to her about trying to take more satisfaction in her accomplishments, such as being asked to work with more senior level analysts when she was still a junior analyst, and to try to take off some of her self-imposed pressure. I was a little worried that she'd consider my words as criticism that would only make her drive herself harder. But I was glad to see that she seemed to take it to heart, and while I believe that she'll always be a Type A, I think she began to understand that she did not have to be a "super analyst."

 6 Comment on your observations of the applicant's ethical behavior.

Ethical standards are obviously important in every field but particularly so in this industry, whose reputation has suffered so badly from a lack of ethics among many powerful people in the world of finance. Not only did Min show a consistent pride in her work and its integrity, but once, after a business trip, I saw from the expense account that she turned in how very modest her expense claims were. This is an area where it is very easy to take advantage; I can't imagine Min ever doing so. Similarly, I am confident based on my knowledge of her that when she rises to greater levels of responsibility, she will hold the best interests of investors above her own.

 7 What do you think motivates the candidate's application to the MBA program at Columbia Business School?

Min understands that to fulfill her long-term career goal of being an investment advisor with a large firm, she needs more formal education and background in business. And with her level of intelligence and ability for hard work, it's only natural that she would aim for a top school such as Columbia. I am confident based on having worked with her for two years that her multifaceted abilities, including a winning personality, will make her outstanding management material.

 8 In what ways could the applicant improve professionally?

I think Min's perfectionist streak, which I described above, is the one thing I would change about her if I could. However, I also understand much of this is an ingrained cultural trait, but I hope that as Min matures as a person and as a professional, she will learn to accept her already excellent work productivity and habits as better than just "good enough."

 9 If you could change one thing about the applicant, what would it be?

I believe my answer to Question 8 covers this.

 10 Are there any other matters which you feel we should know about the applicant?

I had the pleasure of attending a modern dance performance where Min was a member of the troupe. It was delightful to see a completely different and creative side of her emerge. I know how much a school like Columbia values well-rounded applicants, and in addition to her love of dance, Min is also a history buff and regularly devours biographies of famous women in history, such as Abigail Adams and Susan B. Anthony. I asked Min to keep me posted on what she had read most recently, and I borrowed a few of her books from time to time. Frankly, I never figured out how she had time to read so voraciously. I gather she doesn't sleep much.

I plan to keep in touch with Min even though she no longer works for me. I know that she plans to use this time between jobs constructively, and I believe she is planning to enroll in one finance class this summer as well as a writing class. I have no doubt that soon, one lucky brokerage firm will benefit from having Min on their team.

✓ *What works*

The writer of this LOR very obviously likes Min personally, in addition to respecting her abilities highly. Specifics throughout strengthen the recommendation, from the writer having argued with management to keep Min despite a company restructuring, and noting her ethical character, evidenced in part by Min's modest claims on an expense account. Min's weakness of a perfectionist streak is also tempered by evidence of her ability to handle constructive criticism in a mature manner, and of an overall trend toward greater confidence.

12 Tips for Recommenders

1. *Only write the letter if you really care.* Compelling and effective LORs are written by people who truly know and are enthusiastic about the applicant and his aspirations. If you cannot give a sincerely enthusiastic endorsement based on personal experience, do not write the letter. An apathetic LOR will do more harm than good for the candidate.

2. *Ask the applicant for a list of suggested topics/experiences to write about.* LORs should not merely repeat information and anecdotes the applicant has already written about elsewhere in the application. Minimally, they should provide a different perspective on events discussed in the essays. Ideally they would discuss events not discussed elsewhere and also provide the recommender's perspective.

(3) *Give some context for each anecdote that you write about.* This will help the adcom understand and appreciate what the applicant's strengths or achievements were in the situation you are describing.

(4) *Don't pretend the applicant is perfect.* A LOR is not meant to be a fawning portrayal of an idealized candidate, and you will be asked to discuss areas where the candidate can improve. As long as the weaknesses appear reasonable and the overriding impression is that of a highly qualified individual, these answers will help, not hurt, the candidate. Naturally, avoid magnifying the candidate's weaknesses.

(5) *Avoid vagueness and generalities that could be written about almost anyone.* "Katie always goes the extra mile to get the job done" isn't as meaningful or memorable as "Katie's willingness to work overtime when our department project ran behind schedule got us back on track and proved her commitment to getting the job done right." If you make a claim that the candidate has great communication skills, or sense of humor, back it up with an example.

(6) *Highlight strengths relevant to MBA programs.* If you are recommending someone who doesn't work in a highly analytical area, try to write about situations that highlight his intellectual or analytical abilities.

(7) *Don't answer everything unless you can do so fully and meaningfully.* If you don't have good examples or answers for every question on a LOR form, aim for substantial examples for 75 percent of the questions. Don't let the process overwhelm you. On the other hand, when at all possible, write enough about the candidate so that it's clear that you know him well and admire his many qualities and abilities.

(8) *Go beyond checking boxes.* Recommenders who only put check marks in a grid and do not write explanatory notes will hurt the applicant's candidacy. A quick box-checking

exercise will reveal that you did not care enough or know enough to provide helpful, thorough answers. Additionally, since most people who agree to write LORs will give above average marks in the boxes, these grades will mean very little without written answers illustrating the candidate's qualities, skills, intelligence and experiences.

(9) *Write answers of appropriate length.* Skimpy, too-short answers will not add any new knowledge; long-winded answers may offer more detail than desired. Answers to questions can vary in length, but each one should add a new and specific insight about the applicant's character, abilities, management potential and strengths.

(10) *Show how the applicant fits the program.* Ask the applicant for information that states the program's values and character. This will help you write about his personal qualities in a way that reflect those values and help the adcom decide if the applicant is a good fit.

(11) *Pay attention to grammar and spelling.* The applicant has invested a great deal of time, effort and money into getting his essays into highly polished and correct form. If you are less certain of your spelling or grammar, have it reviewed for errors.

(12) *Submit the LOR on time.* Submitting the form late can needlessly slow down or imperil the application.

The Bottom Line

→ **Recruit LOR writers who know you well and care** about your professional aspirations. Unquestionably, detailed letters written with enthusiasm by a midlevel manager trump apathetic letters from a CEO or CFO.

→ **Make the task of your recommenders easier** by providing them with helpful tools, such as a list of achievements/qualities you would like highlighted, relevant work evaluations, your essays and how you are trying to position yourself with the school.

→ **Encourage your recommenders to write with specifics** to make your achievements and character come alive.

→ **Give recommenders the 12 Tips for Recommenders**, in addition to other supporting material, for further guidance.

Prepare to Shine During Interviews

" Be yourself! Don't try to be something you are not. This is not the time to show that you can do everything by yourself. "

" Arrive on time (early if possible) and dress profession-ally! If you sweat, bring a handkerchief to wipe sweat from your brow or your hand. Offer a good, strong, dry handshake and high energy. "

" Always stay positive, even if you are speaking about a failure, mistake or achievement. Never cut down an employer, peer, subordinate…anyone. "

"Make sure your hobbies/interests in your resume are close to your heart so that you can show your passion for them. "

"The person who does 80 percent of the talking feels bet-ter about him/herself. So make sure you have questions at the end so that the interviewer can speak about his/her experience with the program. "

"Get prepared. Try to cover any gaps that may appear on your resume. They do indeed pay extra attention to the flow in your resume. "

– quotes from Accepted.com MBA interview feedback database.[8]

---

8   http://www.accepted.com/mba/interviewfeedback.aspx

Why are interviews important?

If you receive an invitation to interview, congratulations! You've cleared another hurdle and are now one vital step closer to an acceptance. Making it this far in the application process proves that all the hard work you have invested into planning and composing an outstanding application has paid off. But while an interview invitation is an exciting and significant milestone, it also can induce a case of the jitters, occasionally severe enough to require a call to your physician to request a prescription for Xanax. After all, communicating your qualifications to the school *on paper* allowed you time for revisions and edits. In person, once words have flown out of your mouth, "do-overs" become awkward.

It's easy to understand why interviews are important to the schools. In the end, despite your impressive application package, nothing can substitute for live contact to get a sense of who you are. Accepted editor Natalie Grinblatt Epstein, who is a former admissions director at the University of Michigan's Ross School of Business and at the Cornell Johnson School of Business, observes, "If candidates could win me over with their sophistication, passion, energy and charm, I knew would feel comfortable putting them in front of my faculty, alumni, corporate partners and venture capitalists. Even if I suspected that they were not as clear on their post-MBA goals as they had written in their essays, I knew they could learn what they'd need to learn and find the direction they would need to find if they could tell their story in a clear and concise way, using examples, showing energy and doing their homework on my school."

Will your live persona match the one you carefully crafted on paper?

During an interview, you will reveal your authentic self through tangible and intangible qualities. These include the substance of your responses to questions, the quality of the questions you ask, as well as your body language, eye contact, fluency and tone of communication, and overall disposition. Just as your letters of recommendation affirmed who you are via an objective third party, your interview will affirm that the live candidate matches the persona you so carefully cultivated on paper.

But MBA Smarties benefit from the interview process as well. If your interview is a positive experience and your interactions with staff and students on campus (if that is where you will interview) are enjoyable and encouraging, your decision to apply to that school will be affirmed. On the other hand, if the experience on campus is not what you had hoped or the atmosphere not what you expected, you may conclude that another school is a better match.

Schools also interview candidates so that their admissions process does not seem formulaic. This is underscored by those schools that sometimes conduct "blind" interviews, in which the only information the interviewer has about you is your resume. One reason for this policy is to avoid an interviewer being unduly swayed in your favor by knowing about your 780 GMAT and two pending patents. Conversely, schools want to avoid negative bias among interviewers on behalf of some apparent weaknesses on a resume. Interviewers conducting so-called blind interviews are not always totally in the dark, however. They sometimes have instructions from the admissions office to inquire about particular areas of concern. For example, a gap in employment of several months may be hidden on a resume, but not on the application data form.

Natalie adds that good chemistry between an applicant and interviewer is often the magic ingredient, though admittedly not one for which you can prepare. A good feeling about the applicant's personality is even more critical with student or alumni interviewers, who may be asking themselves, Can I see myself working with this person on a team? Can I imagine hiring this person?

Three keys to successful interview preparation

There may be an element of luck as to whether you and your interviewer will click, but there's no luck involved in preparing for the interview in every other way. Throughout this book I've emphasized the importance of knowing your goals, knowing the schools where you apply, and knowing yourself. Finding where these points converge is essential for a successful MBA candidacy, and it remains true as you gear up for your interviews. To perform as effectively as possible, you must remain as fluent about your reasons for obtaining an MBA, the reasons for choosing this particular school, and your goals, as you were when writing your essays. For this reason, when you enter the interview phase, know three things and know them cold:

1. Know how you fit the program and why you belong there.

2. Know yourself.

3. Know the school.

Know how you fit the program – You already have demonstrated your fit with the program substantially in your application, and yet, you will be asked to cover that ground again in your interview. Review your notes from your initial school research. That hard work will pay extra dividends now, reminding you of all the reasons this program stood out to you in the first place. Don't stop there, however. Revisit the school's website to refresh your memory about how your own professional and educational background matches the school's methodology, strength, and career opportunities. Review your essays again (yes, those too!) so when you have coffee with your interviewer, you have total recall about the programs and curriculum that drew you to the school in the first place. This is especially important since interviewers are likely to ask questions that are meant to test your commitment to that school. For example, they may ask if you are accepted to this school as well as your other top choices, why would *this* MBA Program suit your professional needs best?

Dawna Clarke, Director of Admissions at Tuck, explains what schools are looking for in terms of fit in the interview process: "Schools are looking for people who've done their research and are going about this decision using some insight and good judgment about what it is that they're looking for and what that school has to offer. There are so many good schools out there, and you want to convince your interviewer or your admissions committee that their school is a good bridge between your past and your future plans. The best way to make a compelling case is to really show that you know what the school has to offer and what you have to offer the school."

Sometimes, applicants are caught short during interviews, especially when they are asked for more specifics about how they will contribute meaningfully to the program. One client named Liam told his interviewer at Chicago's Booth School of Business that he was excited about joining Net Impact, a community service club, but when the interviewer asked him a follow-up question about whom he had spoken to in the club and which of their current initiatives he found most appealing, Liam was stumped. He hadn't actually spoken with anyone in the club and couldn't remember their current initiatives, though he had seen some examples online during his research. Mortified, he explained that he was "in the process of getting that information."

One stumble like this is unlikely to derail an otherwise solid interview, and naturally, nobody can anticipate every question that an interviewer might ask. It is also unrealistic if not impossible to speak with an active member of every club you're interested in at every program to which you apply. Still, a little contact can go a long way. In this case, for example, if Liam hadn't been in touch with anyone from Net Impact but had talked to someone in the Marketing Club, he could have said, "I'm in the process of making contact with students in Net Impact, just like I did with Sara Smith in the Marketing Club, who told me about initiatives A and B, which would be perfect for my career goals." That would have helped to sidestep his lack of knowledge about the particulars of that club and its activities. Do your best to contact students at your top-choice programs, especially those involved in studies or activities you're aiming for. This way, you can mention these specific interests with enthusiasm and confidence, ready to bolster your statements with references to deep research and some communication with current students or alumni.

Know yourself – The interview is about you, not only professionally, but personally. One Harvard applicant noted on her resume that she had a passion for singing, and was actually asked to sing during her interview. Be careful what you write about in your essays or list on your resume regarding personal interests, or your interviewer may ask you to sing, too!

Tuck's Dawna Clarke also advises all candidates to approach their interviews with a strategy for what they most want to reveal about themselves, especially when going into a blind interview: "So many candidates are bright and impressive, and there are probably 50 things that they would love to talk about to us in their interview. But there's limited time, so I recommend that they choose five of their top skills, experiences, or accomplishments that they most want to emphasize." It's also crucial to be armed with examples to substantiate each of your top points. Ideally, a few of the top experiences or accomplishments on your list will also be those where you had the opportunity to demonstrate traits that are valued by that school. This will underscore that you have fit as well as qualifications.

My company, Accepted.com, has a database of feedback from hundreds of MBA applicants who reported on their interview experiences.[9] Surprisingly, many report that questions they found the most difficult to answer were the ones they should have been prepared to answer even in their sleep. These include talking about a weakness in your profile, what your plans are immediately post-MBA, how you personally have contributed to your team and explaining a career change. None of these questions should take anybody by surprise. At this point in the process, they should not be difficult to answer. These are all part of knowing yourself and knowing how the program fits into your professional goals and matches your personal style. Like the motto of the Boy Scouts, "be prepared."

Know the school – Does the school you are interviewing for value innovation? Leadership? Teamwork? Challenging conventional thinking? Most top schools claim that they value all of these qualities, but some emphasize one more than another. Understand those differences. Understand how the schools define the qualities they value, and be prepared to speak knowledgably about how they try to put these qualities into practice and how you will too.

For example, Duke's Fuqua School of Business has expanded its focus to global innovation and research, with campuses in five international regions. They also have begun partnerships with other established Duke programs on the environment, global health and public policy. If you are interviewing at Duke, show your awareness of this expansive global focus and how you fit there.

What you should ask and what you shouldn't

You will also have time to ask your interviewer questions, which is a golden opportunity to show that you have thought about the program, and your role in it, carefully and deeply.

Good, thoughtful questions of a staff member, student or alum might include: "What changes do you anticipate may be coming to the program in the next year or two?" "If you had to do it again, what would you do differently?" "What advice do you have for a first-year student?" "Tell me more about the school culture." In addition to looking for deeper knowledge about how the program will help you achieve your own educational and career goals, you should bor-

---

9   http://www.accepted.com/mba/interviewfeedback.aspx

row from President John Kennedy's famous line: "Ask not what your MBA program can do for you; ask what you can do for your MBA Program."

Just as there are good and thoughtful questions that will add to your desirability, there are also questions that are considered a waste of time and likely to annoy interviewers. These include asking anything that is readily knowable from the program's website as well as questions about housing and recruiting.

Mention substantial achievements that aren't in the essays

(Did I mention I just climbed Mt. Kilimanjaro?)

One client of ours had trouble finishing his application because he was preparing to lead a team climbing Mt. Kilimanjaro. While he managed to slip the application in under the wire, he obviously could not talk about this fascinating experience in which he acted in an important leadership role. We advised him to mention this trip during his interview because the experience not only reflected well on him, but would certainly make any interviewer sit up straighter and hear what he had to say.

You may not climb Mt. Kilimanjaro before your interviews, but try to bring something of interest to discuss. It may be a new development since your application, or it could be another life experience that shines a light on your career goals or values that you didn't have room to discuss in your essays. For example, one client was only nine years old when she began an antipollution campaign in the poor neighborhood where she was raised. There was no room for that back story in her goals essay, but this experience revealed that her activism began young and had immediate results.

Make sure to work in relevant information about important developments that have occurred since you submitted your application: an improved GMAT score, an A in a business-related course, a promotion, or leadership of a work-related or community service initiative. This is particularly important if you are interviewing at schools like Harvard and Wharton, which have records of discouraging or not accepting new information from applicants after the application submission date -- even if the information is highly relevant and/ or the applicant has sat on the waitlist for months. Relating these new details strengthens your profile overall and shows you as a dynamic individual whose talents and achievements continue to blossom.

Taking a swing at the oddball question

If you were an instrument in our orchestra, what instrument would you be?

You may not break a sweat over the questions you can reasonably expect, such as being asked to walk the interviewer through your resume or relating a challenging situation and how you overcame it. You may be forgiven, however, if you lay awake at night wondering what kind of puzzling and seemingly irrelevant curveballs may be thrown your way. At Harvard, for example, some applicants have been asked the following: "Imagine the HBS classroom was an orchestra. What kind of instrument would you be and why?" "If you had 30 seconds to speak to the United States as a whole, what would you say and why?" "What is one product you can't live without?"

Natalie Grinblatt Epstein observes that these off-topic (to put it kindly) questions are most often asked by alumni interviewers, not adcom staff members. "I don't think it matters as much what you say as how you back up your answer," she notes. "Really, they are looking to see how quick you are on your feet. Weird questions, when they arise, are really more about wanting to see your thinking process and what's important to you." In any case, most people are not victims of Rogue Interview Question Syndrome, so try not to let it worry you.

Behavioral versus qualitative questions

MBA applicant interviews used to focus mostly on general, open-ended, qualitative questions. "Tell me about your leadership experiences," "What three adjectives would your friends use to describe you," and "Tell me about the major decision points in your career so far" would all fall under this category. More recently, though, schools are trending toward asking more behavioral questions, such as "Tell me about a time when you struggled to achieve a goal," "Tell me about a time you received constructive criticism" and "Tell me about a time your team struggled to achieve a goal."

Implicit in these questions are other questions: "What did you do in those circumstances?" and "What was the impact of your decision or response?" As you can see, more self-analysis is required to answer these sorts of questions. You can gracefully move from the qualitative to the behavioral question by referring to the Know Yourself section, above, and Dawna Clarke's recommendation to select five experiences to highlight. On index cards or a spreadsheet, write down the top five character traits that you applied during each of those experiences. Then, think about which character traits are most highly prized by each schoo, and hoe you demonstrated those traits in the experiences. Using this approach will also enable you to back up your claim of being a good listener, team leader, or someone who takes initiative, by showing how you did those things in your proudest achievements. As in your essays, you are not simply making a claim: you are backing up that claim with credible evidence. Also be prepared to go deeper into the stories you have told and to tell additional anecdotes, if called upon to do so.

Finally, a handful of schools (Kellogg and Duke among them) offer open interviews as part of the overall application process – you do not need to wait for an invitation. Make no mistake: applicants who jump at the opportunity for an open interview earn immediate bonus points. Making the effort to get to that campus, even if it's far from where you live, displays a serious commitment by the candidate to the school, and the school will treat that individual's candidacy more seriously in return. This is especially true of candidates living in the country where the school is located.

Recipe for a relaxed interview

Anxiety won't help you prepare for your interview, and if you can't shake it off at the moment of the interview you won't come across as you should or could. Remember that the interviewers sincerely want to get to know you and are not trying to trip you up. Follow these steps to prepare for a relaxed and successful interview.

(1) *Deep breathing.* Learn some deep breathing exercises to help calm you down if the thought of the interview unnerves you.

(2) *Mock interviews.* Practicing with professional consulting staff or friends who are current MBA students or alumni will help you sound completely and thoroughly knowledgeable, but not scripted. Record yourself during the mock interviews so you can hear if you ramble or have too many "ums" or other verbal tics.

(3) *Assess impact of accomplishments and failures.* When reviewing significant experiences you may discuss during an interview, ask yourself, "What have I gained from this experience? What happened as a result of it? What would have been different had I not accomplished this?"

(4) *Be fluent about goals.* Be prepared to answer the following questions confidently and in a heartbeat: What are your short-term goals? What are your long-term goals? What do you hope to gain from attending this program? What will you contribute to your peers? To society?

(5) *Refresh your knowledge of the school.* You want to prove not only that your interest in the school is heartfelt, but also well-reasoned. Establishing fit with the program of your choice means knowing yourself and your goals as well as knowing the program.

(6) *Use the STAR method* (describe the **S**ituation or **T**ask; **A**ction you took, and **R**esults you achieved). This will help direct your answers for common behavioral questions on leadership, team experiences, and goals. Stay within the framework and do not go off on tangents.

(7) *Speak with current students and alumni.* This will bolster your current knowledge of the program. Mine available information about the interview process through Accepted.com's MBA Interview Feedback database, ClearAdmit's wiki, and applicant blog posts.

Using Positive Imagery to Shine During Your Interview

by Sachin Waikar, Ph.D., a psychologist and former admissions consultant with Accepted.com.

In the conference room I imagined myself standing on a tennis court: I tossed the ball into the air then smashed an ace serve right past my opponent. Back in real life, I smiled to myself when the assistant came to tell me the McKinsey partner was ready to meet with me. With confident steps, I followed her down the hall to one of my final-round interviews with the strategy consulting firm.

So why was I thinking about tennis when I could have been recalling business frameworks and other concepts to prepare for a likely grueling case interview? For one, last-minute cramming—and anything done frantically—rarely adds value. More importantly, I was using positive imagery to boost my confidence for the interview. Imagining myself doing something in which I had proficiency—tennis, in this case, which I played for my high school team—endowed me with a greater sense of capability as I approached a less familiar and typically anxiety-provoking situation.

Much research has documented the effectiveness of positive imagery, and it's used for a variety of purposes: excelling in sports, quitting bad habits such as smoking, even experiencing a less painful childbirth process. Many studies have demonstrated the ability of positive imagery, or guided imagery, to help patients deal with medical conditions ranging from allergies to heart disease.

How can you use imagery to prepare for your interview, whether it's for college, graduate school, or a job? First, you should practice the technique before you really need to use it. Start by finding a quiet space in your day, clearing your mind, and using one of the techniques below. The more you practice, the more easily you'll be able to summon imagery when needed. Then, ideally starting a day or two before the interview, practice using imagery to relax yourself and boost your confidence. There are severalspecific ways to use positive imagery:

☑ *Visualize yourself doing something you excel at:*
    This is the version I used to prepare for my consult-

ing interviews. Think of something you're really good at, whether a sport, an academic subject, cooking, or whatever, then visualize yourself doing it. Use very specific details: imagine the setting, the equipment you're using, the result, even the positive reactions of others.

☑ *Visualize yourself excelling in the interview itself:*
If you've been through successful interviews, use your memory of those to help create positive images about the upcoming interview. Imagine yourself shaking hands with the interviewer and providing poised and compelling answers to the questions. Imagine the interviewer nodding in response and giving you positive feedback at the end. Focus more on what this will look like than the content of the questions and answers.

☑ *Use positive affirmations:*
People have mixed feelings about saying positive things to themselves—it can feel forced, corny, or ridiculous to talk to yourself in this way (thanks in no small part to Al Franken's Stuart Smalley character on the TV show "*Saturday Night Live*"!). But you find it helpful to say things to yourself (out loud or in your head) like, "I'm going to do well today" or "I deserve a place in the Class of 2013." There's strong evidence that it works: In controlled experiments, people using positive affirmations were able to lift more weight or break boards more easily than those who weren't. Hopefully you won't have to break boards as part of your interview, but consider experimenting with positive affirmations, with or without any imagery.

Positive imagery helped me get the McKinsey job, and it can help you excel in your interviews.

The Bottom Line ←

→ **Be ready to answer questions about short- and long-term goals** and why you are applying to this program fluently and confidently.

→ **Review the school's website extensively** so that you are 100 percent current with philosophical and academic trends. Try to contact students involved in studies or activities you're interested to show your commitment to learning about the school.

→ **Choose a few of your top skills, experiences or accomplishments** you most want to emphasize during interviews, and/or something new and substantial that's changed since you applied.

→ **Be prepared to ask your own questions** that show substance and thought during interviews.

→ **Engage in mock interviews** to sound thoroughly knowledgeable, but not scripted.

→

Chapter 10

Tips for Special Applicants: Waitlisted, Reapplicants, Career Changers, Military, Overrepresented Groups, Underrepresented Minorities, Older Applicants, Younger Applicants

WAITLIST

Can you turn a "maybe" into a "yes"?

Landing on a waitlist is more nerve-wracking than being on stand-by for a flight. Your bags are packed, you're excited to go, but you don't know if you will make the flight. It's frustrating to have been waitlisted, but look at the bright side: You were a close contender, and the school is seriously interested in you. Most top-ranked schools will not offer feedback on why you were waitlisted. They rely on you to assess what aspect of your profile was a little shaky, if any. Fortunately, you can still make your final argument on behalf of your candidacy through an effective waitlist letter and additional letters of support, if the school accepts them. These will reaffirm your commitment to the program and your worthiness to join the class. I have had the great pleasure of watching many of my clients make their cases successfully and take their seats in the next class at their waitlist school.

Act like a pro, not a prima donna

Unfortunately, sometimes waitlisted applicants let their anxiety or disappointment get the better of them, and they react emotionally, much to their detriment. Increasingly, admissions directors are writing about this problem in their blogs, noting the uptick in emails, phone calls or even visits to their offices by waitlisted applicants who behave in ways that are demanding, rude, disrespectful of their time or otherwise inappropriate. These responses do not demonstrate perseverance; they reveal immaturity and lack of judgment. Randall Sawyer, former Assistant Dean of Admissions at Cornell Johnson, explained how detrimental this is to candidates in a Q&A with me, posted on our blog[10]: "In every phone call, every email, every conversation with students, we are judging you and evaluating you. Whether you come across as unprofessional or professional, or if you come in the office or call and are rude to my staff, we take note of that. There are a lot of eyes on you every time that you contact the office. Use this knowledge to empower yourself to be professional to everyone from the receptionist to the file managers."

Soojin Kwon Koh, Director of Admissions at the Ross School of Business, underscored this same point in her admissions blog in May 2011[11], "Every interaction that an applicant has with a school is considered in our admissions decisions - from the way an applicant treats our receptionist to the communications he/she has with members of the Ross community at large, not just the admissions staff who are perceived as the gatekeepers to the school. If in doubt about whether you should hit the 'submit' button on a note (or an application for that matter), let it sit for a day or two and review it again, or have a friend or family member review it. Will the receiver see your best self in the note or application? If the answer isn't a resounding 'yes,' then you should consider revising it until it is."

Drafting a waitlist letter

If you are waitlisted, follow the school's instructions precisely: Send what they ask for, and don't send what they don't want. If you send in an update, your letter should be short – no more than two pages. Don't dwell on your disappointment at not being accepted or rehash your life or career history. Instead,

---

10   http://www.accepted.com/chat/transcripts/2010/mba10212010_cornell.aspx
11   http://rossblogs.typepad.com/admissions/2011/05/index.html

stay focused on what you have accomplished *since applying*. Your goal for the letter and additional letters of support will be to show the adcoms that you are, in fact, a stronger applicant now than when you first applied.

Open with a brief thank you for continuing to consider your application and reiterate in the first or second sentence your commitment to the school and your belief that its philosophy and approach fit your educational preferences and goals. After this introduction, your waitlist letter and additional letters of support should focus on three critical areas:

 ### Updating your qualifications

Watch me pull an achievement out of my hat!

In the first section of the letter, report any and all substantial achievements since applying. This can include earning a promotion, assuming additional responsibilities or taking notable initiatives in or outside of work. For example, have you taken your department, business or community service organization in a new direction? Have you had an article published? Earned a patent? Launched a business? Succeeded in a particularly demanding class or project? The schools want to admit dynamic, growing individuals, and this is an ideal place to show that you are that kind of person. When possible, highlight new accomplishments not previously discussed in your application. Ideally, you should relate these new achievements to some of the themes or experiences you addressed in your essays.

 ### Steps you have taken to ameliorate weaknesses

If you've really been on top of your game, you will already have begun to address your shortcomings, and in the next segment of the letter, state what you are doing to overcome them. Without specifically mentioning the particular weakness, inform the school of how you are working to strengthen that area. For example, if you enrolled in Toastmasters to improve your communications skills, inform the adcom that you joined Toastmasters two months ago. Tell them what you are gaining from the experience, but do *not* say you have taken this step because you are concerned about your low verbal score or substandard grades. Similarly, if you had a weak academic area, did you take a class in that subject and earn an A? Have you raised your GMAT score? Have you taken a leadership position in community service, which you had neglected since college?

Report other firm and specific plans for additional classes, including when and where you plan to take them. You should also state your willingness to enroll in any additional courses or follow any additional instructions that the school recommends or provides.

Fit with the school

Here it is again: the issue of fit. You may be tired of the subject, but the schools are not. Provide evidence that you belong at that school like a hand fits in a snug glove on a cold winter day and that you will attend if, or should I say *when*, accepted.

You can continue to prove fit by explaining what else you have done to further your knowledge of their program and build your network there. The trick here is to reinforce your commitment to and interest to the school, but to do so in a fresh way that doesn't repeat your essays. For example, you may already have mentioned either in your application or in an interview how the school's philosophy and approach match your educational preferences and goals. In a waitlist letter, cite *new* examples that illustrate this match. For example, what resources have you tapped *personally*, through a conversation or a campus visit? If you have visited the campus (post-submission), mention which class you sat in on, who taught it, and what your impressions were. While on campus, did you chat up some second-years in the cafeteria? If so, give their names, and summarize what they said that resonated with you.

If you exchanged follow-up emails with alumni or students since submitting your application and discovered something new about the program that cemented your interest, say so. Your investment and initiative in connecting with the school, its students and resources will help drive home the message that this school is the best place for someone with your post-MBA goals. More importantly, you will prove that you are continuing to engage their program and its participants.

Schools do respond to this extra personal effort, provided that your sincerity is matched by an equal measure of professionalism and courtesy. Many top schools may have up to 200 or more applicants on a waitlist, adding to the imperative of being patient and respectful of the staff's time and of their directions about how to follow up. MBA admissions directors want waitlisted applicants to show passion, but not obsessive-compulsiveness.

Finally, if a school offers you a chance for an additional interview while you are still on the WL, grab it. During the fiercely competitive application season of 2009, Peggy was waitlisted by Booth, Kellogg, Dartmouth and Wharton. "Kellogg and Dartmouth both gave me the option of another interview and I made a huge mistake by not accepting that offer, which is why I believe I got waitlisted again a few months later," Peggy recalls. With a nontraditional background in social services, coupled with the extra competitiveness of that year, Peggy was eventually rejected from Booth and waitlisted again at the other three schools. Displaying the perseverance and determination that marks successful MBA applicants, the following year Peggy applied to additional schools and eventually accepted an offer at Duke. "I highly recommend sending schools updates (if you are allowed to do so) and asking for information from alumni with whom you have had contact. Don't give up!"

REAPPLICANT

It's me again, but a new and improved me!

The challenge for reapplicants is virtually the same as for those on a waitlist. Both must redouble their efforts to prove their qualifications and fit with the school. However, reapplicants have a significant advantage over those who were waitlisted, even though a waitlist at least signifies a serious interest in you by the school. That advantage is time. As a reapplicant, you have about a year (give or take a few months) to reenergize your application in every way by seeking and demonstrating career advancement, fortifying any areas of weakness, and continuing to court a particular program. Waitlisted applicants, on the other hand, have only a few months to burnish their profiles.

If you are an MBA Smartie, you will have begun to address weaknesses in your application even before getting that painful ding from the adcoms. This will make you far better positioned to make a more compelling case for admission the second time around. Your first step to recalibrating your candidacy is to determine where your application hit a wrong note. I devoted the first half of this book to laying out a strategy to honestly and comprehensively assess who you are as an MBA candidate, how to identify your goals, and how to find the specific programs that match those goals and for which you are qualified. Often, applicants who didn't get in to any of the schools they applied to either rushed their applications and/or set their sights too high. If you didn't do so the first time around, you must analyze your qualifications against your target schools' average stats and requirements. Don't rely on miracles, pixie dust, or a magic wand. Be realistic.

Sometimes, reapplicants become reapplicants not because they are not qualified, but because they failed to present themselves well. Perhaps they rushed. Perhaps they're poor writers. Perhaps they were overconfident and sloppy. Despite the fact that their old essays failed them, many still ask me if they could use those loser essays as the basis for their new applications. The answer is an emphatic *no*. A reapplication is a fresh start; why recycle material that failed to do the job?

Get school feedback if you can

A few schools will offer feedback on rejected applications if asked. For example, USC Marshall School of Business offers telephone appointments to rejected candidates during which an adcom member will help them identify weaknesses. Kellee Scott, Senior Associate Director for MBA Admissions at Marshall, notes that reapplicants to USC Marshall who take advantage of the feedback session most likely become stronger candidates the second time around. "Although reapplicants need only one essay, an updated resume and one letter of recommendation, getting in is not easier," Scott says. "We appreciate the dedication and desire to come to Marshall, but the applicant pool remains highly competitive. Taking advantage of the feedback session and making the necessary changes demonstrates serious interest in our program, which is noted as a positive in the adcom review."

Tina Mabley, Director of MBA Admissions at the McCombs School of Business (University of Texas at Austin), says her school also offers a detailed feedback letter in the summer for rejected applicants who request it, a step that can make a very favorable impression. "Students who take the initiative to ask for feedback are the kind of reapplicants we love to see," says Mabley. "We may have liked the application, but something did not come together. Their skills may not have been well represented, or they may have needed more time for introspection to help them determine fit with the program and goals." Mabley recommends that reapplicants get at least one new letter of recommendation and also warns that a reapplication should not represent a radically different argument for the need for an MBA than was originally offered. Presenting a plan for a career in marketing strategy one year and finance the next will simply raise suspicion. "A reapplication should be a continuation of where you were. The most important thing any reapplicant can do is to have a well thought out plan. Take more classes and interview people working in the industry you want to enter so you can make a stronger case for why you are suited to that industry and a good fit for a school," Mabley recommends.

If you cannot get feedback directly from the school, hire an established graduate school admissions consultant to evaluate your rejected application. If you made mistakes, you need to know what they are now so you can correct them next time. Questions you might want to ask a consultant include:

1. What areas of weakness do you see in my application that contributed to the rejection?

2. Was my work experience MBA quality? If not, what can I do to make it more competitive?

3. Did my essays convey the personal qualities this school values? If not, how can I do better?

4. Did I show enough commitment to this program? Did I explain why I want to attend this school?

5. Did I show clear career direction?

6. Did I show potential to add to the class?

CAREER CHANGERS

In one sense, career switchers are not a special group among MBA applicants, given that well over half of all MBA students fall into this category. The Kelley School of Business at Indiana University estimates that more than half of their students are career changers; MIT Sloan estimates that percentage among their typical classes at 85 percent, and at UCLA Anderson, the Career

Management Center states that up to 90 percent of their students are career switchers, defined as changing industry, function or both.

Still, if you are an IT consultant and making the case for an MBA based on your desire for a career in finance, the burden of proof is on you to show that your interest in finance is a natural and plausible outgrowth of previous interests and experience. As part of that case, you must establish that you not only understand your new field of choice but are temperamentally suited to it as well. For example, if you are that aspiring finance professional moving from IT, can you show that you have the communication and quantitative skills required to succeed in this field, which arguably need to be stronger than in IT? As with all other applicants, your reasons for wanting to earn an MBA at a particular school and for a particular career choice must make sense. You must be well-informed and genuine in your interests and show that you have laid the groundwork for entering a new field.

In the following essay excerpt, notice how convincingly the applicant, Rajesh, makes his case for moving from IT to asset management. As he lays out the steps he has been taking methodically and logically, he makes this transition seem like the most natural thing in the world:

✐ Example: The emerging financial planner

"I first discovered satisfaction in the field of financial planning in India, where I provided basic financial advice to low-income families. That interest grew more serious three years ago, when I had a consulting engagement at Mellon Bank in Chicago. There, my greater exposure to the finance field led me to join an online stock portfolio management competition with Marketwatch. I invested a modest sum and found I loved the challenge and the research involved. I was especially gratified by my results, and today I manage a personal portfolio that has grown to over $60,000, invested in a broad range of stocks. In the past two years I have consistently ranked among the top 0.5 - 2% of all investors with Barron's.

"To further prepare for this change, I have also volunteered between five and ten hours a week with a nonprofit group in Chicago, advising low-income families to reduce their debt, improve credit scores, and even open retirement accounts. In only six months, 80 percent of the families I counseled qualified for credit from banks that wouldn't lend to them

before. I believe that banks can profit from offering essential financial services to the underserved group of lower-income clients, if they are patient
and willing to offer some education in finance. I also believe banks can
expand their retail base at the same time. Finally, I am studying for both
CFA and CMT certifications, which will further my credentials to excel
in your program. I am very enthusiastic about this career transition and
eager to build my career, at least in part, on sustainable enterprise and
helping this neglected demographic to learn essential financial management and investing skills."

From here, Rajesh further clinched his fit and qualifications by noting the
names of classes, clubs, and business simulation labs related to finance at the
schools where he applied. He also mentioned a school initiative at one school
that was specifically targeted to assist low-income groups, an ideal match for
his interests and experience. Rajesh was also able to name students he had
spoken with and observations from campus visits, including references to
conversations with adcom staff, whom he also mentioned by name. You won't
be surprised to learn that Rajesh won a seat at a top-20 school.

If you are a career changer, make sure that your application shows you:

1. *Understand the industry or function you aspire to.* Where and
   when have you worked with people in this industry? What
   experiences do you have that point to your potential to succeed in this function?

2. *Have taken steps to gain knowledge, experience, and a
   network in your new field.* What have you done specifically
   that shows you have been proactive and enthusiastic?
   This preparation could include acknowledging obstacles
   you expect to face as a newcomer to the field as well as
   your plan to address them, thus underscoring both your
   knowledge of the field or function and your maturity.

3. *Acquired skills and knowledge from your previous work that
   will be assets in your new role.* Similarly, show how your
   "different" background will allow you to make a special
   contribution in your new role. For example, Rajesh's IT
   background and experience in technology deployment can

facilitate analysis of a company's true value and potential for continued success. What specialty expertise or skills will you bring to your new field?

(4) *Can articulate your goals as concretely as you can envision them.*

(5) *Know the programs and learning opportunities at your schools of choice* that dovetail with your new career/function choice. Show you have done your homework and showcase your fit with the program.

MILITARY CANDIDATES

MBA hopefuls from military backgrounds sometimes feel insecure in their qualifications because they don't have strictly business backgrounds. Yet these contenders usually have the kind of outstanding leadership experience that MBA programs love. Young men and women in the armed forces who show promise are promoted to higher levels of responsibility on a much faster track than are young professionals in the civilian world. This means that in almost all cases, candidates from the military who are otherwise competitive for leading b-school programs will also have management and leadership experience far more impressive than someone of comparable age with a comparable number of years in private industry.

For example, Brett was only twenty-two, a "butter bar" freshly graduated from West Point when he was put in charge of a platoon of medics overseas, responsible to train them physically and technically. When he became our client a few years later, he had built on this early leadership experience and wrote about the significance, challenges and lessons learned during his military engagements and responsibilities, which included leading 250 Marines in Iraq. Other clients who may only be twenty-five or twenty-six have also led troop deployments overseas, been responsible for procurement or inventory management of more than $30 million of equipment, and had to devise creative technical solutions on a moment's notice when faced with equipment breakdowns in the desert. Working within the vast and often unfathomable military bureaucracy, many have also demonstrated perseverance and innovation in overcoming red tape.

My clients from the military have never lacked for compelling material in their applications. The training in strategic thinking, team leadership, often under life-and-death situations, usually results in applicants who naturally display focus, maturity and a proven willingness to invest long hours to achieve a goal. Their biggest challenge in terms of their MBA applications is learning how to frame their work for Uncle Sam in terms of management and leadership.

How to frame military leadership for b-schools

You can make the most of your military background by writing about experiences that highlight your problem-solving ability, critical and creative thinking skills, and management finesse. Don't forget that the admissions committee readers may not be expert in mil-speak, so don't stuff your resume or essays full of military acronyms that will look like Greek to civilians. Make sure to quantify your achievements: For example, *how many* Marines were in your battalion, *how many* people were in the platoon you led, *how much* the equipment you were responsible for transporting was worth, *how fast* you were able to get an improvised communications system up and running, *how many* platoons other than yours also received commendations for outstanding performance, and the like.

Ideally, military candidates should be able to articulate a logical career vision and fit with a school just like any other applicant. However, given the all-consuming commitment of the military, many candidates simply have not been able to define this vision to the same extent. Sara Neher, Assistant Dean of MBA Admissions at the Darden School of Business (University of Virginia), is more understanding of this fuzziness because military candidates bring so many other strengths to the table. "They have usually led more people than anyone else in their class, and they have also had to deal with interpersonal conflicts in their teams. They are pretty adept at dealing with people in a context that works for business," Neher observes. Still, she advises that military applicants interview friends and relatives in fields they may be interested in to help them assess their suitability for those fields and to help them develop a more directed path.

Many of these MBAs end up in general management or in jobs where supply chain logistics are involved. Several of my clients have been focused from the beginning on growing in management positions within the military itself or in military industries. Obviously, the clearer you are about career goals, the better you can match your goals to the programs. For example, one client who wanted to work within the Department of Defense applied to MIT's Sloan School of Management for its related courses in this area, such as Logistical and Transportation Planning Methods, as well as its Operations Management Club. Internships at Booz Allen Hamilton and the Department of Defense, offered through the Harvard's joint MPP-MBA program, also made sense for this applicant.

Darden's Neher also offers a tip on how military candidates can deal with one other common weakness in their applications: the lack of extracurricular activities. While this is also understandable, Neher suggests that applicants note the humanitarian or mentoring work they have done during their military service on their applications. "Don't just leave those boxes blank if you helped deliver food to the needy while on the base in Kandahar or mentored a younger recruit," she says. "This also counts."

The strengths that military candidates bring to their MBA applications far outweigh their weaknesses. In fact, Neher notes that in the last three years, Darden graduates from the military had a 100 percent employment upon graduation. Those who can qualify for the GI bill also have great incentive to apply: Current rules provide for payment of all in-state tuition up to $47,000, and many b-schools, including Darden, waive application fees for military applicants and also offer some scholarship assistance.

For further information on MBA programs that offer special support for military applicants, and for targeted networking among veterans with MBAs, check out militarymba.net and mbaveterans.com.

OVERREPRESENTED APPLICANT GROUPS

Are you a male, Indian guy in IT? Management consultant? Finance wonk? If so, you may be worried that you fall into one of the dreaded Overrepresented Applicant Groups, the equivalent of ubiquitous Starbucks cafes that cannibalize the sales of other Starbucks down the street. Try to cast that worry aside. First, you cannot change what you are, nor should you try to. Instead, focus on what makes you an individual with traits, abilities, experiences, and vision that are uniquely yours. Remember, if the admissions committee looked only at general applicant groups and numbers, they wouldn't ask you for essays, letters of recommendation or interviews. They would simply request your census information, a transcript and maybe your MBA resume.

The purpose of the admissions process is to help the adcoms get to know you as a human being beyond labels. However, given the number of applications they receive from overrepresented applicant groups, and despite their best intentions, they might be forgiven for sometimes tending to view you at least in part according to stereotypes: the driven, stress-junkie, numbers-crunching finance guy or the quiet, tech-happy, code-writing IT guy. It's your job to show the adcoms that you defy easy categorization and that you are a one-of-a-kind individual with something special to add to the class.

How you can avoid being lumped in with your "group"

To distinguish yourself, you must focus on ways you will contribute to the MBA classroom mosaic and, beyond that, to your intended field. What are your special strengths and talents? Ideally, these will be skills and traits that fall outside the stereotype of your group. For example, you may be extremely creative, a born teacher, or someone with a passion for innovation. Pick one or two of your special, distinguishing traits, and weave examples of them into your essay narratives. If you are not sure exactly what sets you apart, ask yourself: what three or four adjectives would your closest friends use to describe you? What adjectives do you want the admissions committee members to think of after reading your essays? Once you have identified those adjectives, look for examples where you can illustrate those traits in the context of your stories. This will help create a memorable and identifiable picture of you as an individual, not as a member of "that" group.

You can also distinguish yourself by ensuring that the vision you sketch goes beyond the basics. What impact do you hope to have through your work? What will that impact look like, either in your company, your product line or in society? Painting a career vision that is as specific as possible and based on your experiences and realistic assessments of trends in your field will also help you stand out from the competition.

It's often tough for IT candidates to convey the significance of their professional accomplishments without appearing overly technical. For this reason, IT applicants must be able to show at least some experience with and talent for working with people in addition to computers. Specifically, look for instances where you can show strengths in these areas:

1. **Leadership** – Getting buy-in on your ideas, smoothing out interpersonal dynamics and friction among co-workers or team members you manage, convincing management to try a new way of doing things, and the like.

2. **Communication skills** – Show results of winning sales presentations made to customers, at trade shows, or to staff or management at company meetings and quantify those results. Proving leadership will by definition require you to show how well you have communicated your ideas to others, but if you have taken other steps to bolster your communication or presentations skills by joining Toastmasters, volunteering to give presentations, and the like, make note of it.

3. **Nontechnical innovation** – Show how you think outside the cubicle through ideas you have introduced that are related to sales, marketing and team building.

4. **Sales skills** – If you have had ideas for new products, successfully sold a product, been part of a start-up where you also had experience in sales, make note of it.

As a male Indian software engineer applying to MBA programs, Devak was determined to show his business side and transcend the stereotype of an introverted guy sitting in front of his computer writing code eight or nine hours a day. "I didn't have the chance to be in a managerial or customer-facing role," Devak recalls. "Instead, I knew it was imperative for me to take significant initiatives at work and carve out a module or project for myself." Devak took initiatives not only for software improvements, but also to show that he could communicate new features to customers. In this way, he was able to display leadership and communication skills, both hurdles for his profile.

However, he realized he could not rely solely on his work experience to impress the adcom. "I knew that being a cricket captain would not count as memorable extracurricular activity, since almost every male Indian Software Engineer lists 'cricket captain' on his application. My extra-curricular had to be a WOW!" Knowing this, Devak assumed leadership roles in professional networking organizations, recruiting speakers, organizing events, and otherwise displaying impressive leadership and communication skills.

Even as part of an overrepresented group, only you have lived your life

Similarly, investment banker applicants know that their quant skills are unquestioned, but how to show their creativity, their individuality, their softer side? Cindy Tokumitsu, Accepted.com editor and author of the ebook *The Finance Professional's Guide to MBA Admissions Success,* has helped countless clients from a finance field distinguish themselves through both professional and nonprofessional activities.

"As an investment banker you may be overrepresented, but your experience in investment banking is still unique to you," Cindy explains. "To distinguish yourself at work, dig into the details of your experience. Show what drives your interest in the field. That story is yours alone. It defines and illuminates you as an individual. For example, you may be captivated by the dynamics of the transactions, but someone else might love the business of evaluating markets and conceiving new products. Yet another person may have gravitated toward the entertainment industry and wants to specialize in that niche. These three different people will have totally different anecdotes and examples to share, and the results will be three completely different and completely engaging commentaries."

You can also display your individuality from your nonwork activities, but remember, the *why is more important than the what in MBA essays.* That means you will need to go beyond talking about what you did and uncover the insights gained in the activities you have been involved with. Show that you are a growing, dynamic individual, shaped in part by what you have learned from your work and nonwork activities. This will add depth to your candidacy and fight any tendency among the adcoms to view you as part of a stereotype.

"If you are involved in the arts, sports, or an intellectual discipline, for example, portray it in your essays," Cindy adds. "If you're a violist in an amateur string quartet, don't just explain how your leadership enabled the ensemble to thrive. Write about your love of music and what it means to you to have that dimension in your life." Your personal background may also be a way to distinguish yourself. "If you're from a farming family in Iowa, the adcom would sure love to know how you ended up at Goldman Sachs in Manhattan. If you discuss experiences from your personal background, though, be sure to demonstrate through example and anecdote their formative influence on you."

Look for the unexpected story angle

For any applicant, but particularly for those from heavily populated applicant groups, it's vital to look for the unexpected story angle. For example, an essay from an IT guy about how he worked nearly round the clock one weekend to root out the bugs that were causing software failures in a new software package, therefore enabling the product to still launch by its promised delivery date, would show the kind of determination and smarts they already expect from this profile. But writing about what he also learned about the process of discovery, or how a friendship with a coworker unexpectedly blossomed during that stressful period, would add a fresh dimension. An otherwise ordinary tale could become extraordinary and memorable.

Every year, thousands more highly qualified individuals from IT and investment banking apply to top MBA programs than the programs can possibly admit. Distinguish yourself from the competition through the distinctness of your experiences. Look for the experiences in your life where you can introduce the skills and character traits you possess that that belie the stereotype of your group so that you will emerge as a compelling, engaging and irresistible candidate.

UNDERREPRESENTED MINORITIES (URMs)

Diversity remains a top priority on college campuses, and business schools realize that they need to ramp up recruitment of underrepresented minorities (African-American, Hispanic and Native-American) who can grow into the ranks of business management. Still, in 2010, just over 7 percent of all full-time MBA students attending the fifty top-ranked programs hailed from these minority groups, according to Peter Aranda, Executive Director and CEO of The Consortium for Graduate Study in Management (cgsm.org). The Consortium provides career counseling, professional networking and generous merit-based fellowships for MBA students who attend participating member schools and who can demonstrate a commitment to furthering the goals of diversity in their professional lives.

In 2011, seventeen b-schools among the top-ranked fifty were members of the Consortium. Those member schools had 38 percent higher minority attendance than nonmember schools, and between 2003-2010, among top-10 ranked b-schools, only Consortium members (Dartmouth and NYU) boosted their number of URM students, by twenty-seven. All others were down, collectively, by seventy-four.

URM applicants must do the same work as every other applicant in assessing their qualifications and clarifying their goals for an MBA. They, too, should apply to schools where their stats will fall within the 80th percentile of the class average. However, URMs must also evaluate their fit for the program beyond the basics of the curriculum supporting their career goal and learning style, recruitment and campus personality. They will want to know in advance just how much of a minority status they will have once on campus.

Do you have a pioneering spirit, or do you need critical mass?

"If they have a pioneering spirit, URMs may be quite happy on a campus where they are the only one of their ethnic group," Aranda observes. "But they may find themselves in a position where they are asked to speak for 'all' African-Americans, Hispanics or Native-Americans, and most of us don't pretend we can speak on behalf of our entire community." Aranda advises applicants to look carefully at student demographics as well as what sort of clubs, activities, even food and other cultural opportunities exist on campus and in the surrounding community that can help them feel more at home. Schools that are just beginning to expand their minority base will obviously look for those applicants who have that pioneering spirit, but many more students are likely to need a critical mass to thrive.

Often, URMs may not have as competitive GPAs and GMAT scores as nonminority students. With extensive (and often, expensive) GMAT prep increasingly the norm among MBA applicants, Aranda cites what he calls "incredible GMAT inflation" over the past decade that hurts applicants who cannot afford it. Still, b-schools and corporate recruiters put a lot of stock in a GMAT score, which remains a benchmark of how a student will perform in class, especially during the first year. URM applicants should plan to take the GMAT at least twice, and if they cannot afford established prep courses, prepare using lower-cost alternatives such as books with self-tests, CD-ROM courses, and by taking community college quant classes, such as statistics.

Aranda reassures minority applicants that b-schools take a holistic approach to admissions, also looking at leadership potential and extracurricular involvement. Still, while encouraging students to have high aspirations, he and I are in total agreement that students must choose schools consistent with their qualifications. That means including a stretch school and a safety school among the target list.

EARLY CAREER APPLICANTS

A few years ago a handful of business schools began recruiting younger applicants as a way to ramp up the percentage of women and underrepresented minorities in the MBA classroom. Additionally, these schools wanted to attract ambitious, directed college grads who didn't want to wait to finish their education before jumping onto the grad-school bandwagon.

This trend seems to have passed quickly. Most of the schools who experimented with early career applicants found that the level of focus and maturity they like to see in MBA students is not something that can be rushed. Frankly, it is the rare applicant who could possibly have gathered the kind of life and work experience that leads to a career vision that is authentic, plausible and logical by the tender age of twenty-one or twenty-two. Students who lack this essential foundation and focus can easily get swept up by the tempting plethora of programs and clubs offered by MBA programs, joining them in a scattershot way that wastes these great resources and opportunities. Finally, internship and job recruitment opportunities begin the first year of a two-year MBA program. With minimal work experience, which recruiters will find you appealing compared with classmates who have additional years of valuable experience?

Even if you are that rare applicant who has already started a business, had fabulous internships, and sees a clear career path, you still must do the work of every other successful MBA applicant and take a good, hard look at your qualifications and options. Do you have excellent grades and test scores? Will your work experience, whether part-time jobs or internships, stack up against the competition? Do you *really* know what you want to do after you earn your MBA? Is your target profession open to MBAs with little or no full-time work experience? If you can answer "yes" to all these questions, you might be that singular candidate who is ready with less than two years of work experience. If not, take the time to get a year or two more of real world professional experience, which will undoubtedly focus and clarify your goals further and make you more competitive with top programs.

Still in a hurry? Just can't wait? Check out one-year master's of management degree programs, geared for the early career applicant. Duke-Fuqua, Wake Forest, IE Business School, and London Business School are among the programs offering this degree, but as always, check each school's website for their student profiles to make sure you will be competitive. You may also want to consider HBS 2+2, Yale Silver Scholars and Stanford, which will admit college seniors and defer admissions for specified period of time so that the senior can gain work experience before starting the MBA.

OLDER APPLICANTS

Most full-time MBA students have between three and eight years of work experience, so by age thirty you may be considered an "older" applicant at many schools. Checking listings on *Businessweek* or *U.S. News & World Report* will give you information on student demographics at the schools you are interested in, so you will know at what point you would be considered older -- generally defined as three years older than the average.

Although more experienced students bring additional insights to the classroom, schools are concerned about the greater challenge of older students finding internships and full-time positions after the program. Fortunately, there are many excellent options for the older MBA candidate. If you have ten or more years of work experience and can afford to take off a full year for study, you can investigate the Sloan Fellows Programs, which are run independently at MIT, Stanford and the London Business School. These year-long programs, all of which incorporate an extensive international field trip, are geared for midcareer professionals looking to enhance their general management and leadership abilities. (All are supported by grants from the Alfred P. Sloan Foundation.)

Getting to the next level as a midlevel professional

The largest of these programs is the MIT Sloan Fellows Program, offering either a Master of Science or MBA. While ten years of work experience is a minimum requirement, for the past decade students have averaged around fourteen years of experience, according to Stephen Sacca, director of the program. Leadership ability is a key requirement. "This is not the program for people who are just taking a year off or getting their ticket punched," Sacca says. "We want people with demonstrated leadership skills who know they haven't yet reached their full potential. We seek people who say, 'I know I can do better. I just need the opportunity to think deeply about how I'm going to get to the next level.'"

Similarly, students at the Sloan Fellows program at London Business School also have fourteen or fifteen years of experience on average, according to Balbir Guru, Recruitment and Admissions Manager. They are also looking for applicants who have been "proactive in managing their careers, and are at a turning point where they recognize that this is a crucial year to build skills and knowledge for the next phase," Guru says.

Understandably, many professionals who want to earn an MBA at a mid-career point simply cannot afford to take off a year for full-time study, even assuming they could win a seat at one of these competitive Sloan Fellows Programs. Executive MBA programs (EMBA) are part time and have con-siderably higher acceptance rates than full-time MBA programs. In recent years, more EMBA programs, including some of the highest ranked, such as Kellogg, Cornell, University of Chicago, the University of Michigan (Ross) and UCLA Anderson no longer require the GMAT. Other schools, including the Stern School of Business, NYU, Goizueta and Emory may accept waivers for the GMAT for technical degree holders or those with extensive profes-sional experience. Still, even if you apply to a program where the GMAT is not required, if you have taken it and score highly, report your score. Not only does it prove your academic readiness for the coursework, but it underscores your commitment to excelling in the program as well. A good GMAT could also help compensate for a lackluster GPA still on your record.

While many schools charge a premium for these programs, employers some-times sponsor their midlevel managers in these weekend programs to some extent, rightly viewing it as a wise investment. EMBA programs can be ideal for students in their late thirties to early forties who have managerial experience and who require additional formal education to move further up in management.

Given their ages, many EMBA students already have families and must gear up for a very intense year while they maintain their day jobs, attend school on weekends, and still fulfill family obligations. And since these students are frequently sponsored by their employers to rise within the ranks of their current companies, EMBA programs are less geared to career changers than career enhancers.

There is more variety than ever among EMBA programs in terms of location and schedule. Duke's EMBA program, for example, offers a Weekend Executive program that meets alternate weekends on campus, while its Cross Continent program involves week-long residencies in the United States, Europe and Asia. UNC Kenan-Flagler's weekend option draws students from twenty-two states and offers an evening option, a weekend option, and an option that involves classes once a month, global residencies, and online coursework. Several EMBA programs also partner with global EMBA programs. For example, NYU Stern has a partner program with the London School of Economics and HEC School of Management in Paris to offer the TRIUM Executive MBA.

Precisely because there are more programs than ever, targeted for increasingly specific experience levels and learning goals, you must be clear in your essays about your reasons for selecting these programs and why you are a good fit for them. In addition to distinguishing yourself in your essays, demonstrating your career achievements and articulating your career goals, you need to convince EMBA programs that you understand the demands of studying while working and perhaps balancing family life as well. In fact, some programs have an essay asking you to explain your plan for balancing this overflowing schedule. This is not only because they need to know you can handle the coursework, but because you are also expected to participate actively in the class and add value to the learning community. You can demonstrate this capability by explaining your time management system until this point as well as how you plan to adjust your schedule to incorporate a full focus on school.

The return on investment for EMBAs is a healthy one, according to the Executive MBA Council 2010 Student Exit Benchmarking Survey, released in 2010 by the Executive MBA Council (www.emba.org and www.execu-tivemba.com). This survey of 3,674 students from 116 programs reported increases in their salary and bonus packages from the start to the end of their programs of 11.4 percent, or from an average salary and bonus package of $127,955 at the beginning of the program and rising to $142,534 by the end of the program. Additionally, 37 percent of students in the survey reported receiving promotions and 68 percent reported receiving new responsibilities during their time in the program.

The Bottom Line

→ Waitlisted applicants and reapplicants need to **update adcoms about their qualifications, address profile weaknesses,** and **focus on their fit** with the programs.

→ Career changers must **show proactive preparation for the new path** and what **assets and talents they bring** to the new field or function.

→ No matter what your applicant group, **target schools appropriate to your qualifications and articulate your goals clearly.**

→ Military candidates need to **avoid mil-speak, quantify leadership achievements, and emphasize humanitarian work** done through the military, especially if you have had little time for extracurricular activities.

→ Candidates from overrepresented groups should **emphasize communication, leadership, nontechnical innovation and sales skills** to add distinction. Look for the **unexpected angle** and uniqueness of your experiences.

After You Hit "Send"

You've sent your last application, (I hope more than two minutes before the midnight cut-off for that round!), and now you're undoubtedly breathing a little easier. No matter the outcome, having completed a series of MBA applications in a serious, thoughtful way is a real achievement.

Even with this hurdle behind you, I still have a little bit of advice to help you prepare for your MBA studies and enhance your chances of snagging a great internship, which can lead to a post-MBA job. In the coming weeks and months, try to do the following for a successful transition:

☑ *Look for an internship related to your post-MBA goals.* It's not unusual to feel a little stale and disinterested at work as you wait for this next exciting chapter in your professional life to begin. To avoid just going through the motions until you begin school, ask your employer if he or she can give you an internship or new job duties more closely related to your post-MBA goals. This new role would be especially useful if you are a career changer. Not too many employers have the ability to move you into a new position, but if yours is one of them, seize the opportunity. Not only will you enjoy a valuable learning experience, but your employer will enjoy having a motivated employee until the last day.

☑ *Explore your intended fields.* If you didn't meet with people in your field of choice before applying, it's not too late to benefit from this process now. Set up informational interviews with people in your industry to find out what courses they found most valuable when they were in b-school. Ask about good internship options and typical career paths. While you aren't asking for a job or internship at this point, just information, I have heard of these kinds of informational interviews leading to internships and jobs.

☑ *Unwind.* Financial reality may dictate that you work until the last minute, but if you can swing it, take a vacation or find some other ways to relax and rejuvenate before school begins.

☑ *Plan the logistics of life in b-school.* Don't wait till the day before classes begin to figure out if your furniture will fit in your new apartment. Give yourself enough time to establish yourself in your new town or city, open a bank account, get your internet set up, and figure out other relevant Very Important Places for your lifestyle, whether the best Thai restaurant, the hippest jazz club, or the "*hautest*" hair salon.

And if you have read this book with the intention of applying in several months. . .

I hope the information presented here has given you a broader and deeper picture of how much really goes into a successful MBA application. When you are ready to apply and would like additional advice, please visit my website, Accepted.com, where you will find a wealth of material on all aspects of the admissions process, including special reports, on-demand webinars, and dedicated pages such as:

MBA Admissions 101 - articles with advice as well as Q&As with admissions directors at top b-schools
http://www.accepted.com/mba/admissions.aspx

MBA Sample Essays
http://www.accepted.com/mba/sampleessays.aspx

MBA Interview Feedback Database
http://www.accepted.com/mba/interviewfeedback.aspx

B-School Zones - School-specific information on the top MBA programs that interest you
http://www.accepted.com/Zones/bschools.aspx

Since 1994 I have helped MBA applicants gain acceptance to top MBA programs through individual consulting, editing, and posting myriad resources about MBA admissions on my website. However, sharing general principles, information and insights cannot compare with working one-on-one with clients. In this process, experienced editors with expertise in MBA admissions know how to listen for the nuances of applicants' stories and situations. This, in turn, helps chart a direction to the most effective, clear and distinctive presentation possible.

Furthermore, even professional writers have editors. Writing is improved when a second pair of objective, experienced eyes critiques it. With so much at stake in your MBA applications process, I hope you will consider recruiting one of our experienced editors, too.

Whenever you apply...

Finally, I welcome your feedback on *MBA Admissions for Smarties*, particularly what you found most helpful and insightful. Please let me know how I can make future editions even more effective by visiting http://www.accepted. com/MBASmarties to provide your reactions. And we have a small free gift for you if you do stop by the MBA Smarties' page.

I wish you every success!

About the Authors

Linda Abraham is the founder and president of Accepted.com, the premier MBA admissions consultancy. She is also the co-founder, first president, and current vice-president of the Association of International Graduate Admissions Consultants.

Since 1994, Linda has advised thousands of clients applying to top MBA programs. Her expert personal coaching and editing, as well as the concrete, cogent admission tips she has written on her Accepted.com Admissions Almanac blog and in more than a dozen grad school admissions ebooks, have benefitted countless applicants. As a leading expert in grad school admissions consulting, Linda has been quoted in *The Wall Street Journal, The New York Times, The Sunday Times of London, MBA Podcaster, Beat the GMAT, GMAT Club, Poets and Quants,* and other media outlets and web sites. Linda has an MBA from the UCLA Anderson School of Business.

Judy Gruen joined Accepted.com as an editor in 1996, bringing broad experience in corporate communications, health care public relations, journalism and essay writing to her work with clients. Together with Linda Abraham, she has co-authored two Accepted.com ebooks: *MBA Letters of Recommendation That Rock* and *Law School Letters of Recommendation That Rock.* Additionally, Judy's essays on topics both serious and humorous have appeared in dozens of major media outlets and have been anthologized in several books. She is also the author of several award-winning humor books, including *The Women's Daily Irony Supplement.* Judy has a master's degree in journalism from Northwestern University's Medill School of Journalsim.